COUNTRY WALKS
Cottage Country

COUNTRY
WALKS
Cottage Country

Anne Craik

The BOSTON
MILLS PRESS

Published in 2000 by
Boston Mills Press
132 Main Street, Erin, Ontario N0B 1T0
Tel: 519-833-2407   Fax: 519-833-2195
e-mail: books@bostonmillspress.com   www.bostonmillspress.com

An affiliate of
Stoddart Publishing Co. Limited
34 Lesmill Road, Toronto, Ontario, Canada M3B 2T6
Tel: 416-445-3333   Fax: 416-445-5967
e-mail: gdsinc@genpub.com

Distributed in Canada by
General Distribution Services Limited
325 Humber College Boulevard, Toronto, Canada M9W 7C3
Orders: 1-800-387-0141 (Ontario & Quebec)
Orders: 1-800-387-0172 (NW Ontario & other provinces)
e-mail: cservice@genpub.com

Distributed in the United States by
General Distribution Services Inc.
PMB 128, 4500 Witmer Industrial Estates, Niagara Falls, New York 14305-1386
Toll-free: 1-800-805-1083   Toll-free fax: 1-800-481-6207
e-mail: gdsinc@genpub.com   www.genpub.com

04   03   02   01   00   1   2   3   4   5

THE CANADA COUNCIL | LE CONSEIL DES ARTS
FOR THE ARTS | DU CANADA
SINCE 1957 | DEPUIS 1957

*We acknowledge for their financial support of our publishing
program the Canada Council, the Ontario Arts Council, and
the Government of Canada through the Book Publishing
Industry Development Program (BPIDP).*

Canadian Cataloguing in Publication Data

Craik, Anne, 1938–
Country walks: cottage country

Includes bibligraphical references.
ISBN 1-55046-276-8

1. Trails – Ontario – Guidebooks.
2. Hiking – Ontario – Guidebooks.   I. Title.

GV199.44.C22O58 2000   917.1304'4   C00-930646-3

Printed in Canada
Design by Chris McCorkindale and Sue Breen
McCorkindale Advertising & Design

Contents

Central Cottage Country 81

Rideau Valley 114

Acknowledgments

Many people had a hand in this book. First and foremost, I thank Fergus Craik, my husband and hiking companion for almost forty years, and the many friends who accompanied me on my walks. The fact that we are still speaking to one another is a tribute to their forbearance, stamina and unfailing good humour. I thank them heartily for their comments (occasionally downright unflattering), their advice (not always civil), but above all, for their companionship, which was always lively and never, never dull.

I am greatly indebted to the people who helped me to find and select suitable photographs and to those who took the time to review and correct the text. Special thanks are due to Pat Fleishmann, Georgian Bay Islands National Park; Ron Tozer, Algonquin Provincial Park; Scott Thomas, Massasauga Provincial Park; Bert Koporaal, Frontenac Provincial Park; Christian Barber, author of *Their Enduring Spirit*; Christine Bourolias, Archives of Ontario; Kevin Callan; and Dennis Mills.

Finally, I extend my thanks to the many members of staff in national and provincial parks, and in conservation and recreation areas, who made the task of gathering information much easier than I had anticipated. Without exception, they received me cordially, provided me with pamphlets, maps and brochures, and kept me up-to-date on trail changes and innovations.

Preface

This book grew out of a series of questions posed mostly by cottage-owning friends who wanted to combine cottage life with hiking. The popular impression seemed to be that the two interests were mutually exclusive. Some people were overtly skeptical: "There is more water than land!" "Everything is privately owned!" and "There can't possibly be any decent trails!" were some of the pessimistic remarks I kept hearing. So I decided to rise to the challenge. But, having made the decision to seek out the hiking trails of Cottage Country, I was faced with a problem. Exactly what and where is "Cottage Country"?

"What" is not too difficult to define: the phrase "Cottage Country" seems to conjure up a very special and specific kind of landscape—rugged, forested hills, dramatic outcrops of bare rock, and myriad lakes, streams and rivers. However, "where" isn't as easy to pin down. Where you believe cottage country is depends largely on where you are from!

If you are from Toronto, cottage country is most likely to be Muskoka and Georgian Bay. But what if you are from Kingston, Peterborough or Ottawa? For you, cottage country could be any of a number of areas: the Kawarthas, the counties of Haliburton, Hastings, Lanark and Renfrew, the Rideau Lakes and the French River area (to name only a selection of possible contenders) can all legitimately be called "Cottage Country." Given the vast area that can lay claim to the name, I decided I had to set some practical limits on how much ground I and my hiking companions could reasonably cover. So if my selection seems arbitrary and if I seem to have spurned some obvious gems—Killarney Provincial Park, for example —it is not out of capriciousness, it is only because they are beyond the range of travel I set myself at this time.

The Cottage Country of this book lies on the southern portion of the Canadian Shield, between the Ottawa River and Georgian Bay. More specifically, it sits within the following boundaries: its northern limit is the Highway 60 Corridor of Algonquin Park; the southern boundary follows the south edge of the Canadian Shield between the Severn Sound and Kingston; its western boundary follows the east shore of Georgian Bay, between Penetang and Parry Sound; and in the east, the boundary runs along the Rideau waterway from Kingston to Westport.

Most of the trails are in public recreational areas—national and provincial parks, conservation areas and crown lands. And most of the trails described are loops—hikes that take you back to your starting point without backtracking. The range of hikes varies widely; some are easy, most are moderate, a few are very long and strenuous. I hope the selection will appeal to a wide range of people: novices who have not hiked before but would like to try it; recreational hikers who want to combine hiking with other activities such as fishing, swimming and canoeing; and experienced hikers who are looking for a wilderness challenge.

I have tried to choose trails that pass through scenery that is varied and full of interesting features. Walking through Cottage Country's forested landscape is very pleasant, but if you never emerge from the trees it can get a bit tedious. Many of the trails I have chosen make ascents to high panoramic lookouts or travel across wide, open expanses of rocky terrain that afford long views over both land and water. Others have specific features of interest: several visit dramatic waterfalls or rapids; some can only be accessed by water; a couple visit significant prehistoric sites; and a few take you to totally secluded lakes where you can sit in solitude with only a pair of loons for company.

A great diversity of ecological systems is to be found on the Canadian Shield. The walks will take you along the banks of slow, stately rivers and brawling torrents, through marshes, along the edges of bogs and cedar and hardwood swamps, through coniferous and mixed forest, and over granite ridges. Each of these habitats has its own blend of flora and fauna, so you may experience a tremendous variety of plant, bird, mammal, reptile and aquatic species.

I have been able to make only passing reference to these flora and fauna. If you wish to understand more about what you encounter, take a good field guide and a pair of binoculars, approach wildlife slowly and quietly, and keep a notebook and pencil handy. You'll be surprised how quickly you'll learn to put a name to the sights and sounds around you.

Many beautiful trails await the Cottage Country hiker. Have a wonderful time as you discover them.

Introduction

The Geology of Cottage Country

When you hike in Cottage Country, you'll often find yourself walking on bare, exposed rock. After a while you become aware that an immense variety of shapes, textures and colours lies underfoot. In fact, the bedrock of Cottage Country is the result of over a billion years of geological change and is a jumbled patchwork of rocks that originated in many different ways and in many different places. To give just three examples: near Parry Sound the alternating bands of bright pink and dark grey rock that now form the bedrock were formed 20 to 30 kilometres deep within the earth's crust; near Bon Echo Provincial Park (north of Napanee) pillow-shaped formations in the rocks reveal that they were formed by a volcano that erupted under water; and in Petroglyphs Provincial Park (northeast of Peterborough) native carvings adorn a huge outcrop of white marble that could only have come into being in a tropical climate.

If you are a curious hiker—and I believe that many hikers are—who wants to understand how these very different forms of rock ended up so close together, it helps to know a little bit about how different kinds of rocks are formed and how they move from one place to another.

Classes of Rock and Plate Tectonics

Rocks fall into three basic classes: igneous, sedimentary and metamorphic.

Igneous rock forms when magma (hot molten material from deep within the earth) rises, and then cools and hardens. Granite is the most common igneous rock.

Sedimentary rocks are formed through the erosion of rock particles by wind or water. As these particles settle and accumulate at the bottom of oceans or rivers they form distinct layers, each different from its neighbours. Sandstone, limestone, shale and conglomerate are among the most common sedimentary rocks.

Metamorphic rocks are formed when the earth's crust is subjected to stresses of heat and pressure so intense that some rocks melt and their mineral make-up changes. On cooling, the rock is different from the original—it has metamorphosed into another kind of rock. Granite, for example, metamorphoses into gneiss, shale becomes slate, and limestone becomes marble. With repeated stresses, a metamorphic rock can continue to change.

Much of the bedrock of Cottage Country was baked, squeezed and twisted into metamorphic rock during a period of mountain building that occurred between 1.2 and 1 billion years ago. When, why and how mountain building takes place is determined by a phenomenon called plate tectonics—the constant movement of the vast plates that make up the earth's crust. Briefly, the theory of plate tectonics postulates that the earth's surface is covered by about ten large plates rather like the shell of a cracked, hard-boiled egg. Some plates carry an ocean; others carry both an ocean and all or part of a continent. This jigsaw of plates floats on top of a hot, semi-liquid layer of rock known as the mantle. It is thought that an up-and-down flow of magma in the hot mantle is what causes the plates to move.

Geologists believe that plate movements have cycles. Every few hundred million years, the movements of the earth's plates brings continents together. A supercontinent is formed, then it begins to split apart. This cycle of collision and rifting has been repeated over and over for more than 4 billion years.

The Formation of Cottage Country

Cottage Country lies along the southern fringe of the Precambrian Shield, which contains some of the oldest rocks in the world. The Shield is the nucleus of the continent—the place where it first began to evolve. The small piece of continental crust that was its beginning became larger as new blocks of crust—sediments and volcanic island chains—were swept against its edge. Each new block, called a terrane, was younger than its predecessor and further away from the centre.

The oldest part of the Shield, the Superior Province—land to the north of Lake Superior—was formed 4.5 to 2.5 billion years ago. Between 2.5 and 1.3 billion years ago, the Southern Province formed and attached itself to the south and eastern edges of the Superior Province. Cottage Country, however, is part of the youngest portion of the Shield, the Grenville Province, which stretches southeast from the Sudbury area to the St. Lawrence River. It came into being between 1.8 and 1 billion years ago, in a series of dramatic events that ultimately welded together two separate belts of crust—the Central Gneiss Belt and the Central Metasedimentary Belt.

As their names imply, the two belts contain different kinds of rock. The rocks in the Gneiss Belt—the area between Georgian Bay and Highway 35—are mainly gneiss, formed when heat and pressure metamorphosed older rocks, and granite, formed about 30 kilometres below the earth's surface about 1.5 billion years ago, when hot magma intruded into the crust. The Central Metasedimentary Belt—the area east of Highway 35—contains a mixture of sedimentary and volcanic rocks.

The two belts are thought to have been rammed into each other by a large tectonic plate pushing in a northerly direction. As layer after layer of overridden crust piled up one on top of another, a vast mountain range arose. The end result was an amazing hodgepodge of rocks lying at all angles and in overlapping layers and bands— granite and diorite; metamorphic rocks such as gneiss, marble and quartzite; and volcanic and metavolcanic rocks, such as basalt and greenstone.

Since those major upheavals, geological activity in the Grenville Province has been much less dramatic. However, over the next several hundred million years, uplift and erosion continued until, eventually, the great mountain range was reduced to a low plain. Shallow tropical seas flooded the plain and, between 570 million and 66 million years ago, sediments (mainly limestone) accumulated on the Precambrian base. However, after the seas receded, erosion once again removed most of the sedimentary layers.

But that is by no means the end of the story. Although the basic shape and the lay of the land was determined millions of years ago, the landscape as we know it today was sculpted by a much more recent geological event—the Great Ice Age. Four times within the last 2 million years, glaciers as much as two kilometres thick pushed across most of Canada and into the northern United States. As most traces of earlier advances were obliterated by the final episode, the glacial features we find today in Cottage Country are remnants of the Wisconsin Glacier, which advanced over the area, beginning about 60,000 years ago.

Scouring and bulldozing its way across the continent, the ice stripped vegetation and soil and gouged into the underlying bedrock. It deepened and widened river valleys. Where it encountered areas of softer rock, it dug more deeply, and wherever it went, it carried along with it millions of tonnes of rock, sand and gravel.

The knobs and ridges that today stand up above the general level of the plain have been rounded by ice. Where the bedrock is exposed, its surface has been planed to a smooth finish, except for parallel scratches, or striae, which tell you the direction the glacier flowed.

When the ice finally retreated, about 12,000 years ago, it left solid debris behind. South of the Shield, a blanket of debris—called till—up to 100 metres thick, covers the underlying rock. On the Shield's hard rocks, however, it is rarely more than a couple of metres thick, usually less, and is sometimes nonexistent. But the ice did not pulverize everything. In many places you will find surprisingly large rocks perched on the surface. These are erratics, large boulders that were trapped within the glacier, carried great distances, and finally left abandoned by the retreating glacier on alien bedrock.

Change continued in the wake of the retreating ice. Vast amounts of meltwater poured forth from decaying glaciers and formed huge lakes, forerunners of the present Great Lakes, in the Michigan–Huron and Georgian Bay basins. For a time, one of these lakes, Lake Algonquin, inundated the Georgian Bay basin as far east as Huntsville. When the waters retreated, hundreds of lakes remained in the low areas, while along the shoreline, bare, scoured and polished rocks stood exposed as a lasting testament to the power of those ancient swirling waters. Elsewhere across the Shield, as the glaciers melted, they left behind myriad lakes and swamps in basins gouged out of the less resistant bedrock.

Rivers also changed their character. Over time they carved new valleys, cutting through soft glacial deposits until they eventually reached hard sills of Precambrian rock. No longer did they flow smoothly along a ramp-like course; they now tumbled precipitously from rock basin to rock basin via the dramatic waterfalls, rapids and chutes that have become such a distinctive feature of the Cottage Country landscape.

Of course, change never stops. Imperceptibly the landscape will erode as wind and water take their toll, gradually wearing away soil and rock. But with any luck, over next few million years, the sweeping ridges, wooded hills, and lakes, streams and waterfalls will remain, and Cottage Country will continue to be a dramatic and strikingly beautiful place to walk.

The History of Cottage Country

The hiker in Cottage Country will encounter many local features that give one place a character that is quite distinctive. Nevertheless, there are many shared characteristics, particularly of physical geography, flora, fauna, and human history. When you are on the trail it helps to be aware of some of these common threads.

First and foremost is the area's physical appearance, sculpted by the action of the glaciers upon the porridge of ancient bedrock. To be sure, there are variations: the land gets hillier and higher as you move north, and the lakes vary greatly in size; some areas are dominated by chains of very large lakes, others are peppered with small ones. But wherever you walk, you will encounter a combination of the same physical features: rivers, lakes, swamps, forested rolling hills and rocky ridges. In most places the ground is covered by a thin veneer of glacial till, but sometimes even this meagre cover is absent.

Glacial till was an important factor in Cottage Country's human history. Where it was absent or minimal, vegetation was meagre or nonexistent, but if there was a little depth—usually not more than two metres—it proved to be an ideal growing medium for trees. Throughout Cottage Country the same patterns of growth occurred: where the soil was moist and gravelly, hardwoods proliferated; dry, sandy, outwash plains were dominated by the giant pine; and spruce, fir, cedar and hemlock covered the low-lying and wet areas along lakeshores and in valley bottoms.

Humans discovered a rich diversity of wildlife on the Shield. For many centuries, nomadic native peoples hunted and fished in its abundant forests and lakes. Europeans were latecomers; it was not until the beginning of the seventeenth century that European explorers, missionaries and *coureurs du bois* finally began to traverse the region. But travel through Shield country remained sporadic, and thorough exploration did not take place until the nineteenth century.

Finally it was the need for safer and better lines of communication between the St. Lawrence River and Lake Huron that stimulated exploration of the inhospitable, isolated lands of the Shield. After the War of 1812, the fear of continuing American hostility prompted the search for a water route to connect the Ottawa River and Georgian Bay. Between 1819 and 1836, a number of expeditions struggled up and down the rivers that flowed east, south and west from the Algonquin highlands. Each expedition encountered similar

*The challenge of the Shield—watercolour, entitled
"A cabin in the woods," by Millicent Mary Chaplin, 1838-42.*
Source: National Archives of Canada, c 921

obstacles: rough, rugged country, and rivers impeded by falls, chutes and rapids. Eventually, the notion of a navigable waterway had to be abandoned.

The expeditions, however, were not in vain. The explorers were quick to realize that the great virgin forests, so difficult to travel through, were a potential source of immense wealth. Little time was lost. By the 1830s, logging companies had reached the east side of what is now Algonquin Park; by the early 1840s, the forests alongside the newly completed Rideau Canal were under assault; by 1860, forests from the Ottawa River to Georgian Bay resounded with the sound of the saw. The logging boom lasted until the 1920s, by which time the usable timber was depleted. Today's forest is almost all second growth; only occasionally will the hiker encounter a small, isolated stand of first-growth trees. Burned-over stumps and bare-rock ridges are all too prevalent reminders of the loggers' progress.

Wherever the loggers went, settlement followed, and although the government had reluctantly abandoned the idea of a navigable canal across the Ottawa–Huron tract, the notion of opening up the land remained very much alive. To some extent, the enthusiasm sprang from an assumption, made by the explorers, that soil that produced magnificent trees must be suitable for agriculture. Some of the surveyors sent to assess the land for settlement potential were far less optimistic, but the government, undeterred, pressed on with grandiose plans for roads to take settlers into the Ottawa–Huron tract.

As it turned out, the problems were legion: rocks, lakes and hills made straight lines impossible, creeks required bridges, and swamps needed a hard causeway. A few roads were completed. Some were abandoned. Nevertheless, by 1870, a network of roads, some running north-south (the Frontenac, Addington, Hastings, Burleigh, Bobcaygeon, Victoria and Muskoka Roads) and a few running east-west (the Mississippi, Monck, and Peterson Roads), extended into the southern part of the Shield. They brought hopeful settlers onto free lands offered by the Province of Ontario and enabled the logging companies to expand their operations into inaccessible areas. Today, some of these old Colonization Roads carry busy highways; others, long abandoned, lie hidden in the bush, a sudden and poignant reminder to the hiker of the hopes and hardships of an earlier era.

The success or failure of a settlement depended on many factors, but one of the most important was the quality of the land that awaited the settler. Where there was some depth of soil, there was hope of survival, and if the homestead was situated where extra income could be gained from logging or mining, hope was higher. There were, nonetheless, many settlers who found the rocks, the isolation, the harsh climate, the bad roads and the endless trees too much to bear. Toward the end of the nineteenth century, when the West was beginning to open up, the speedy exodus from the Shield was serious enough to be referred to as Manitoba Fever.

In general, when a settlement was sited on land with tillable soil, close to a usable road, or better still, at a crossroads and near a waterfall which could easily be harnessed to provide power for saw and grist mills, it had some chance of success. And if it had a navigable waterway in the vicinity, its chances were increased.

In the eastern part of the region, the construction of the Rideau Canal between Kingston and Ottawa gave a great boost to settlement and commercial logging and mining operations. Following the opening of the canal in 1832, thriving mill towns and villages sprang up all along its course.

The same was true of Muskoka. Alexander Cockburn, an entrepreneur, was quick to recognize the commercial potential of the area's large lakes. His steamboat service on Lake Muskoka began in 1866. The construction of locks and a short canal quickly opened up all three Muskoka Lakes to commercial navigation. By 1878, boats were operating on Muskoka's northern lakes, from Port Sydney

Oliver's Ferry - Rideau Lake - looking towards Bytown.

*Rideau Ferry, on the Rideau Canal, 1834—one of a series
of 114 watercolours by Thomas Burrows,
Assistant Overseer of Works for the Rideau Canal.*
Source: Archives of Ontario, C1-0-0-0-25

through Huntsville, west to Làke Vernon, and east to Peninsula Lake to connect, via a stagecoach, to the Lake of Bays.

In the last two decades of the nineteenth century, Muskoka's lakes teemed with commercial traffic. Steamers took passengers and freight to villages and carried vacationers to the many resorts that were appearing on the lakeshores. (Muskoka in fact had a large resort hotel at the head of Lake Rosseau as early as 1871.) Tugs towed huge booms of logs to sawmills. By the end of the century these commercial craft had been joined by the luxurious private yachts of wealthy summer residents.

In the many parts of Cottage Country where water transportation was not feasible, travel and transportation remained fraught with difficulty until the advent of the railway in the latter years of the nineteenth century. Profitting from the continuing expansion of the logging industry and the establishment of significant mining operations, railroad entrepreneurs succeeded where road builders had failed. By 1900, they had pushed rail service northward through some of the most isolated and rugged parts of the Shield to link the

A log boom on a Muskoka lake awaits the drive down-river to the sawmills.

Source: Archives of Ontario, Acc 2203 S 3667

Making the wilderness accessible.
The OA & PS railway travels through the bush, ca 1890.

Source: Algonquin Park Museum Archives #74, J. W. Ross.

communities of Huntsville, Haliburton, Bancroft, Renfrew and Westport. Of the lines that ran from east to west, the most famous of all was the Ottawa, Arnprior and Parry Sound Railway, built by lumber baron J.R. Booth.

Without a doubt, the railway had a profound effect on the economy of the Shield and on the lives of its inhabitants. Trains carried lumber, minerals, produce and people. Towns and villages sprang to life along the railway's many routes. However, the boom was short-lived. By the 1920s, both mining and logging operations were on the wane, and the economy of towns dependent on these industries began to dwindle.

But by that time, boat and rail transportation had already begun to open up the Shield to sightseers. The wild and rugged beauty of the remote northern landscape obviously impressed them, for tourism quickly took hold. The Muskoka Lakes boasted 76 resorts by 1909; Bon Echo Hotel, on Mazinaw Lake opened in 1899; Highland Inn in Algonquin Park opened in 1908. As the railways proliferated, so did the vacationers and, by the 1930s, the wild and lonely lakeshores and rock-strewn lands that 70 years earlier had filled the settler with dismay and fear, now bristled with resorts and cottages.

After the Second World War, a rapidly improving highway network generated a further expansion in the cottage population of the southern Shield. An economic boom created a more affluent, leisure-oriented community. The challenge for governments was no longer how to get people into the wilderness; it became a question of how to save at least some of the southern Shield from being totally overrun.

One obvious solution was to create more parks. But this proved to be a formidable task. In 1954 Ontario had just eight provincial parks, with only one—Algonquin—in Cottage Country. Several years earlier, Algonquin's superintendent had reported that the park's campgrounds, childrens camps and resorts were suffering from the effects of overuse. The situation was deemed critical, and the parks division of the Department of Land and Forests had already launched a provincial parks expansion plan. In some areas the search for potential parkland was fruitless. Around the Muskoka and Kawartha Lakes any suitable, sizable expanse of land was already developed, with property values sky-high. But away from these areas, undeveloped land could still be found. In 1959, the government acquired a highly desirable 480-hectare property which bordered both sides of the narrows on Mazinaw Lake. (This tract would later become Bon Echo Provincial Park.) Cottage Country's second park, Killbear Provincial Park, came into operation in 1960, and over the next ten years the parks division managed to acquire parcels of land for each of the provincial parks that feature in this book.

The success of the land acquisition program was very closely tied to the emergence of an increasingly vocal environmental movement. In fact, the role that environmentalists played in the creation of the present provincial park system cannot be overestimated. The passion and intensity of their fight to protect and preserve our natural heritage helped bring about a profound change in the public's attitude. One practical consequence of the resulting change in priorities was the rapid expansion of the provincial park system during the 1960s, '70s and '80s. Even more significant was the fact that park policy gave precedence to protection of natural features; development of recreational activities became a secondary, strictly regulated objective.

The provincial parks discussed in this book cover 800,000 hectares of land and water. With an additional 50,000 hectares of Conservation Authority and Crown lands, hikers in Cottage Country have a lot of ground to explore and hundreds of kilometres of hiking trails to guide them through it.

We should all be grateful that these parks and trails exist, and we must guard against complacency. We live in an era of shrinking public funding and increasing privatization. The links that provincial parks are now forging with the private sector may or may not be a good thing. It is up to us to see that the natural treasures that are protected now remain protected in perpetuity.

Using This Book

Cottage Country is divided into four hiking regions—Algonquin Provincial Park, Georgian Bay's Eastern Shore, Central Cottage Country and Rideau Valley. The text for each region opens with a general introduction, which is followed by a section on each park or recreation area within that region. A summary at the head of each chapter gives information about the trails. Each trail to be featured is shown in **bold type** and accompanied by details about the type of trail (loop or linear), its length, the time it requires, and its level of difficulty. There is also advice on how to get to each park, where to obtain trail maps and brochures, and where to park your car.

The time calculated for each walk is obviously an estimate and should only be used as a guide. It is based on the assumption that your reason for hiking is largely to experience and explore the natural beauty of the landscape, in which case, your progress will be steady rather than hurried. So, I have I estimated that you will cover no more than, and sometimes less than, 2.5 kilometres an hour.

All distances—in the text and on the maps—are approximate.

Each walk is classified as *easy*, *moderate*, or *strenuous*. An *easy* hike is one that is fairly short, travels over mostly flat or gently rolling terrain, and follows a well marked, unobstructed trail. A *strenuous* hike, by contrast, is longer, with many ascents and descents, and goes over rocky terrain. A *moderate* hike falls between the two. Don't attempt a hike labelled *strenuous* unless you are a fit and experienced hiker.

Trail markings differ from park to park, but all the trails are marked—sometimes by blazes and/or posts, sometimes by icons, and occasionally, in rough and rugged country, by cairns. On only a very few hikes are the trails difficult to follow.

Most of the detailed descriptions are accompanied by a sketch map. Many parks and recreation areas publish interesting and informative leaflets, some with excellent trail maps and explanatory details. I urge you to make use of them. In many cases they add immeasurably to what I have only been able to mention.

The hikes I have included for detailed description are the ones I happen to like best, but this selection comprises only a fraction of the hiking trails available. In each chapter, however, I have tried to make brief reference to the overall range and scope of trails to be found in any particular park. Also, a short section at the end of the text on each region gives highlights of other notable trails in that region—railway trails, resort trails, wilderness trails, township trails and trails in private recreation areas—that are not in parks or on public land.

In a few cases, I have made specific recommendations about where to stay. These comments are confined to places that I have visited personally. However, because this book is about Cottage Country—and Cottage Country is all about vacations—I have tried to include some general guidance about accommodation. At the end of the book you will find information about camping facilities in various parks, where to call for advice on B&Bs and other places to stay, and how to find a cottage to rent.

A final note: please remember that trails can change. A severe winter storm may cause damage that necessitates the temporary closure of a trail. Industrious beavers may wipe out a trail, or a trail may be rerouted for conservation reasons. The same applies to trail markers; from time to time, trail markers are replaced, often in a different place. My descriptions, to the best of my knowledge, are up-to-date. However, if you encounter a discrepancy, the markers and blazes on the trail always take precedence.

Hints for Hiking Safely

Obviously, trail conditions will vary according to the season and the weather. It is up to you to exercise good judgment and take appropriate precautions for your own personal well-being. Here are a few simple guidelines.

- Always prepare ahead for a hike.
- Make sure you have adequate clothing and footwear—boots are necessary for all but the easiest hikes.
- Take an extendible (telescopic) walking stick, available at many outdoor stores, to help you negotiate rocky, steep, and flooded terrain safely.
- Carry essential articles (see below) in a day pack .
- On the trail, modify your speed in inclement weather and take extra care if the path is rocky or where it follows a cliff edge.
- Avoid hiking alone, particularly in more remote areas. If you must hike alone, give someone your route and timetable.
- If you lose the trail, try to retrace your steps to the last marker. If this fails, sit down. Have something to eat, then look at your map and concentrate calmly on where you may have gone wrong.
- Remember that Cottage Country is blackfly and mosquito country. From May to the middle of August, carry an effective insect repellent—one with a high concentration of DEET. Or you may prefer to wear a bug shirt—obtainable from many outdoor stores.
- Treat all drinking water obtained on the hike, except the potable water that is available in some parks and conservation areas.
- Give wild animals a wide berth and never get between a mother of any species and her young.
- If you are camping in a park interior, always hang your food, soap and toothpaste in a bag on a line strung between two trees, about four metres above the ground and away from your tent. Do not take your backpack into your tent, since it may smell of food.

Day Pack Essentials

- Rain suit or waterproof and windproof jacket
- Sweater
- Hat (for sun protection or warmth) and gloves
- A change of socks
- Water bottle (1 litre per person, per day, 3 litres in summer)
- Lunch and some high-energy snacks
- Compass and whistle
- Insect repellent and sun screen
- First-aid kit, and moleskin felt to prevent blisters
- Trail map
- Small flashlight
- Swiss Army knife

Cottage Country Hiking Areas

Sketch Map Index

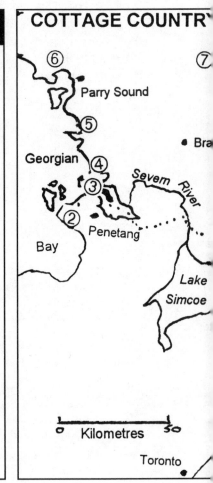

COTTAGE COUNTRY

Parry Sound

Georgian

Severn River

Penetang

Bay

Lake Simcoe

Bra

Kilometres

Toronto

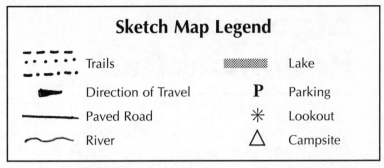

Sketch Map Legend

・-・-・	Trails	▨▨▨▨	Lake
►	Direction of Travel	**P**	Parking
————	Paved Road	✳	Lookout
～～～	River	△	Campsite

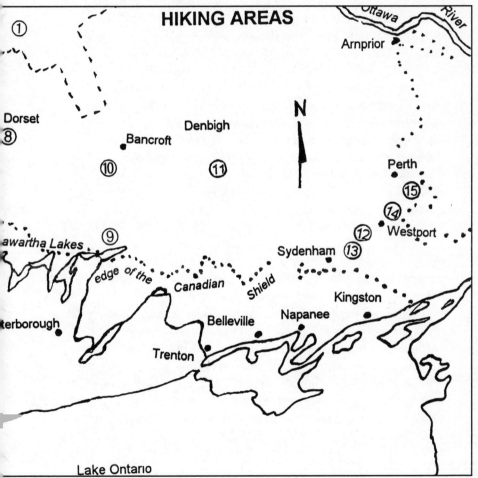

HIKING AREAS

Ottawa River

① Arnprior

Dorset
⑧ Denbigh
Bancroft
⑩ ⑪

N

Perth
⑮
⑭
⑫ Westport
awartha Lakes ⑨ Sydenham ⑬
edge of the Canadian Shield
Kingston
erborough Belleville Napanee
Trenton

Lake Ontario

Algonquin Provincial Park

Algonquin Park can aptly be described as both the crown and the cradle of Cottage Country, so it is a fitting place to begin this book. It stretches out over the top of the Algonquin Batholith, a huge dome of granite that was once buried 20 to 30 kilometres beneath the earth's surface. This dome now lies exposed on the surface, rising to a height of 577 metres above sea level. This is Cottage Country's highest land and its oldest bedrock.

There is another very good reason to begin this book in Algonquin Park; its seemingly endless forests and sparkling waters make it the epitome of Shield country. And there is more. For many people Algonquin is an almost mystical place; the name alone often evokes a memory of a profound emotional experience. Whether it is the memory of the haunting call of a loon, early mist rising off still, clear water, or a sea of hardwoods aflame in the autumn sun, Algonquin, once experienced, seems never to be forgotten.

Ontario's oldest park has not always been as tranquil as it is today. Over 107 years it has seen many changes and its eventful, often controversial, history vividly reflects a profound change of attitude—on the part of governments, policy makers, and the public at large—toward the natural environment.

Today, we readily accept the fact that carefully defined limits and restrictions are a necessary part of environmental protection. Algonquin, however, came into being in a very different era—at the height of the settlement and logging boom—when nature was seen as a force to be tamed and exploited, rather than to be protected. The park was not created to protect the wilderness; it was created for a very practical reason—to protect the headwaters of several rivers.

As logging and settlement spread, unchecked, across the Shield, two provincial government officials, Alexander Kirkwood and James Dickson, became very concerned about the long-term effects of clearing the Algonquin Highlands. They suggested that land be set aside to preserve the natural forest cover and protect the headwaters of the major rivers. In 1893, after due consideration, the Ontario Legislature passed an Act that set aside 3,755 square kilometres of

Settlement in the Algonquin Highlands.
A settler's hut along the Opeongo Colonization Road.
Source: Archives of Ontario, C120-2, S5056

land to provide a "public park, and forest reservation, fish and game preserve, health resort and pleasure ground for the benefit, advantage and enjoyment of the people of the Province."

Protect the trees, protect wildlife, encourage recreation—the ideas sound so modern and conservationist. But what exactly did they mean in 1893?

If you take a brief tour of Algonquin's history by glancing through *A Pictorial History of Algonquin Provincial Park* (published by the Friends of Algonquin Park for the park's centennial in 1993), you'll get some idea of how different was the notion of conservation at that time. There are some astonishing images of the park's early years: vast areas laid waste by logging, lumber mills, a railroad crew blasting its way through rock, a hotel with a billiard room and a dance pavilion, and park rangers posing in front of drying beaver pelts.

These pictures are a vivid reminder that in 1893, conservation was not about preservation of the natural environment. Conservation

*Advertisement for Algonquin Park,
published in* Rod and Gun *magazine 1911.*
Source: Algonquin Park Museum Archives # 2667, Canadian National Railways

Algonquin Provincial Park

was about using the natural environment: using it wisely and well, and above all, profitably.

So, there was never any intention to halt logging (the lumber barons supported the idea of the park because it got rid of competition from settlers). Lumber was perceived to be the park's most lucrative resource, and the railway was viewed as a most efficient means of exploiting that resource. Fish and game were also seen as valuable resources—"surplus" beaver turned out to be one of the most profitable "crops."

Economic exploitation of Algonquin's natural beauty soon followed, early in the park's life. By 1913, the railway's passenger service was booming; carrying the well-to-do to luxurious "wilderness" vacations at the park's five resorts, young people to youth camps, and vacationers to their leased cottages.

Throughout its first fifty years, resource exploitation and recreational expansion remained the park's major goals. The concept of preservation was not totally absent, but it didn't really come to the fore as a serious issue until the 1940s, after the completion of Highway 60.

Suddenly, the park became accessible to the masses rather than only to the favoured few. As tourism boomed, a host of problems surfaced. Overcrowding, noise and pollution gave rise to fierce debate over the park's primary function: was it recreation or preservation? The most bitter confrontation, however, turned out to be over logging policy. On one side was the rapidly expanding preservationist movement, which saw logging as nothing less than a desecration of the natural environment; on the other were the logging companies, determined to preserve the status quo.

After many years of bitter controversy, slowly but surely, the doctrine of "use and profit" was superseded by the doctrine of preservation. Out of the long-unresolved conflicts, there emerged a strong environmental movement, and by 1974 the preservationists had won some major battles—particularly in the regulation of recreation. Motor boat traffic, interior camping and canoeing were all subject to much tighter restrictions. Logging was regulated by being put into the hands of a single crown corporation, the Algonquin Forestry Authority, and limited to about 75 percent of the park's area. All logging was banned in primitive, natural and historic zones and felling in the rest of the park was subject to strict controls. Finally, after more than eighty years, Algonquin had begun to look and feel like the zoned and regulated park we know today.

Algonquin's trails bring you face to face with its past. However, the reminders of its early years are fading rapidly as nature reasserts itself. Silence now reigns in the places that once reverberated with the blast of dynamite, or echoed with the sound of the saw. And today, if you are fortunate enough to catch sight of a beaver or a moose, you can enjoy the privilege, secure in the knowledge that they are not going to end up on anybody's back or mounted on a wall.

Today, there are two distinct Algonquin environments—a result of the construction of Highway 60. The Interior remains accessible only by canoe or on foot; the Highway 60 Corridor is accessible by car.

To explore the Interior on foot, you must hike along one of three wilderness backpacking trails—two accessible from Highway 60, the third accessible from the Achray Campground on the east side of the park. The various loops along each of the trails take between 2 and 5 days to complete—campsites designated especially for backpackers must be reserved in advance. These trails, which afford an opportunity to explore the very heart of Algonquin's wilderness, are for fit and experienced back-country hikers. They are beyond the scope of this book. But if you are interested, a very informative and detailed topographical map of the backpacking trails is available from the East and West Gate Information Centres.

The Highway 60 Corridor is, of course, the area that receives most of the park's visitors. Here you will find picnic areas, campgrounds, beaches, museums, and lodges. It most certainly is not wilderness; whatever the time of year, you will encounter people on the trails. But if you are happy with a less daunting but nonetheless memorable experience, the Corridor, with its 13 day-hikes, has a lot to offer.

One bonus of the Corridor is that the wildlife viewing opportunities are equal to and sometimes better than those in the Interior. In spring, sodium-starved moose gleaning salt from the roadside ditches are a common sight along the highway. You will rarely see wolves, but you may well hear them at night, particularly in summer, when the pack brings its pups from their dens to areas called rendezvous sites. (If you are in the park on Thursdays in August you can join a Wolf Howl.) And if you sit quietly by the side of a small lake or pond in the late evening, you might be rewarded by the sight of a beaver going about its nightly business.

The trails along the Highway 60 Corridor vary in length from 0.8 to 13 kilometres, and each one explores a different aspect of the Algonquin environment. The ones described here just happen to be my favourites. Two very short ones serve as an ideal introduction to the park—that is, if you are one of the few people reading this book who have not yet been to Algonquin. These two trails also leave you enough time to call in at both the Visitor Centre and the Logging Museum.

Highway 60 is marked according to the distance from the west gate of the park, km 0, to the east gate, km 56. In all the park's literature, points of interest along the Corridor are defined according to these distance markers. The same system is followed in this book.

The Visitor Centre, at kilometre 43, is an excellent place to start your visit to Algonquin. Opened in 1993 to commemorate the park's centenary, its wonderful location and design make it feel like an integral part of the landscape. A viewing deck opens onto a breathtakingly beautiful panorama of forested ridges, lakes and a huge bog, and inside, uncannily realistic displays depict the park's major habitats with their characteristic flora and fauna. There is also an excellent bookstore and a restaurant. A little to the west, at km 39.7, the Lookout Trail takes you to one of the finest views in the park, and the Beaver Pond Trail, at km 45, does just what you would expect (although it is best undertaken at twilight if you want to catch a glimpse of the residents).

The Algonquin Logging Museum, just inside the east gate, at km 54.7, vividly recreates the park's long logging history through a series of exhibits placed in chronological order along a 1.3-kilometre trail. A replica of an early camboose camp, an alligator (an amphibious tugboat used to move logs across lakes) and a log chute are just three of the mementoes that trace the evolution of logging techniques from the 1830s to the present.

Two of the three other trails, the Centennial Trail and the Track and Tower Trail, take a full day to complete. Both are rugged and demanding and should only be attempted by hikers who are reasonably fit. Booth's Rock Trail is shorter and less arduous, and can certainly be completed in half a day.

Five Algonquin Trails

Trail Information: There are 13 trails along the Highway 60 Corridor. The five trails described here range from 1.9 to 13.2 kilometres. A series of numbered posts guides the hiker around each trail.

Lookout Trail—1.9-kilometre loop, 40 minutes, moderate
Beaver Pond Trail—2-kilometre loop, 40 minutes, moderate
Centennial Ridges Trail—10-kilometre loop, 5–6 hours, strenuous
Track and Tower Trail—13.2-kilometre linear trail, 7–8 hours, strenuous
Or—7.7 kilometre loop, 3-4 hours, moderate
Booth's Rock Trail—5.1-kilometre loop, 2–3 hours, moderate

Access: Each of these trails is accessed from Highway 60. You must stop at either the East or the West Gate to pay an entrance fee.

Map: A park brochure that shows the location of each trail is available at the East and West Gate Information Centres. Interpretive guides for each trail are also available at the Centres and at each trailhead.

Parking: At each trailhead.

Lookout Trail

From the parking lot at km 39.7, the trail takes you immediately up into tall, airy woods dominated by birch, maple and hemlock. After a few minutes you descend to a stream, which you cross via a wooden bridge. Shortly after, when the trail forks, take the right-hand branch.

The path ascends over rocky ground, past an enormous boulder, once carried along by the glacier and left high and dry on this spot when the ice retreated 12,000 years ago. It doesn't take long to reach the top, and after a short, sharp climb, you emerge from the forest onto a broad, west-facing rock shelf.

Rugged pines stand guard on the edge, patches of lichen and moss cling to the rock face and, in the shallow pockets of soil just slightly further back, the white flowers of bunchberry and the delicate foamflower bring a touch of colour to the starkness of the cliff. The views are spectacular. Directly below, the hardwood canopy forms a dense sea of colour; in spring a subtle blending of myriad shades of green, in fall a glowing mosaic of yellows, reds and the darkest of greens. The land spread out in front of you, some of the highest in the park, is part of the crown of the Algonquin Dome. Elevations reach as high as 585 metres above sea level, and at least eight major rivers have their headwaters here. The Madawaska rises only a few kilometres to the west and, in fact, flows through each of the three visible lakes that add shimmering intrusions of blue to a scene that seems to go on for ever. On a really clear day, you can see hills that are 25 kilometres away.

Once you leave the cliff face, the trail descends quickly through a mixture of white pine and sugar maple. The path is rocky and uneven in places so take care. You will reach the parking area in about 20 minutes.

Beaver Pond Trail

This is another short trail, only 2 kilometres in length but quite rugged in parts. It offers some great views and also an opportunity to examine the habitat of the beaver at close quarters. The trail booklet is very helpful if you want to learn about the life and times of a beaver colony.

Just south of the parking lot at km 45, a bridge takes you over a stream to begin a descent through the trees. After about ten minutes, the trail brings you out of the woods into an open area ringed with a backdrop of dark cedars. In front of you is a large beaver pond with an old abandoned lodge clearly visible. Follow the boardwalk across the beaver meadow at the east end of the pond and, if you stop for a moment, you'll both see and hear that there is plenty of life among the grasses. Once over the meadow, the trail continues west along the shore. Water lilies and bog iris put on a magnificent show in the shallow water, and, if you take a close look at some of the downed trees lying at the edge, you'll see that they support beautiful bog gardens—miniature and aesthetically pleasing arrangements of grasses, iris and sedges.

At the end of the pond, some steps take you up a wooded slope, and then descend again to another boardwalk and a path that follows alongside a stream. A few minutes later, you come to a beaver dam, or rather to two beaver dams; the first is abandoned, but the second, slightly higher up, is a most impressive edifice—a masterpiece of engineering, constructed of sticks, rocks and mud. More steps lead up to Amikeus Lake to a point from which, if you look carefully, you can see about six beaver lodges (not all of them in use). The path climbs again and takes you alongside the lake for about 300 metres before making a sharp right turn. A steep, rocky ascent brings you to a high rocky shelf on the top of a cliff, where you get a great view over the first beaver pond and cedar-ringed meadow, to the wooded hills beyond.

From the lookout, the trail turns north, and a ten-minute walk back through woods brings you back to the bridge and the parking area.

Centennial Ridges Trail

Centennial Ridges Trail is the most demanding of the Algonquin Park hikes described here—and also the most spectacular. It takes you along two parallel ridges, cut through by ancient fault lines. Erosion has deepened and widened the faults into valleys that run at right angles to the ridges and cut them into a series of cliffs. As the trail passes along the edge of five of these cliffs, hikers must be able to cope with a series of quite steep and strenuous ascents and descents with very little level walking. Much of the trail is uneven and rocky, so sturdy boots are a must. Having said all that, let me emphasize that the effort is more than worth it. A good portion of this hike passes through open terrain with unobstructed views of some of the park's most splendid scenery. Whatever the time of year, I can guarantee you will not be disappointed.

The Centennial Trail was opened in 1993, as part of the park's Centennial celebrations. It is dedicated to 11 people who played a crucial part in creating, shaping and developing the park. The trail brochure outlines the role that each played, so if you are interested in Algonquin's history, be sure to pick one up.

From the turnoff from Highway 60 at km 37.6, follow a road

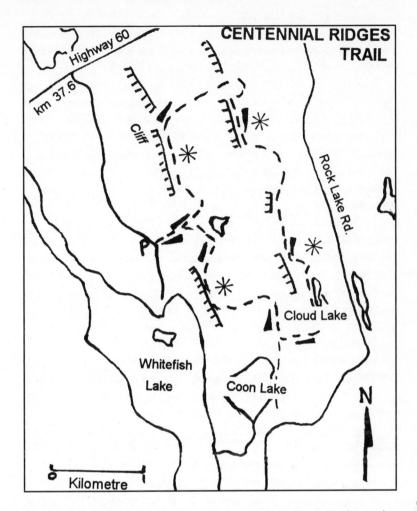

heading south for two kilometres to a parking area. From here, the trail sets out through woods, mostly pine. After a few minutes it passes a beaver meadow where you can just make out an abandoned lodge. A boardwalk takes you over the wet part of the meadow. Beyond the meadow, the trail passes through aspen and birch, bringing you to Post 1 about ten minutes after the start.

From here the trail starts to ascend through trees and over rocky terrain, and after a couple of minutes the path divides. Take the left fork. The trail continues to climb through cool, damp woods composed mainly of large birch and aspen, and carpeted with ferns. After only 15 minutes or so, you arrive at the cliff top and Post 2. This is the first of many spectacular lookouts.

From the edge of a cliff dotted with pines, you survey the treetops of the hardwood canopy directly below. The main body of

Whitefish Lake lies a little to your left; Lake of Two Rivers is a little further off to the northwest; and, beyond that, a seemingly endless series of high tree-clad ridges stretches out to the horizon.

The trail heads north along the ridge, hugging the cliff edge all the while and, as it nears Post 3, you get a splendid view of the wetland at the end of Whitefish Lake. Soon after Post 3 the trail turns sharply to the right and starts to descend. After about 300 metres, you reach a small pond with a beaver dam at its head, and the path goes round the dam, over a footbridge and along the water's edge. Dead trees in the water stand frozen in grotesque and fantastic poses.

Beyond the pond you enter mature deciduous woods and pass through a shallow gorge with rocky sides. Then the trail makes a horseshoe-shaped curve to the right and starts to climb once more, this time through a jumble of very large moss- and fern-covered rocks, until it reaches the top of the second ridge, which is parallel to and slightly east of the first. Post 4 at nearly 560 metres above sea level, is the highest point on the trail and affords similar views to the west and northwest.

The trail then follows the cliff edge south, bringing you to Post 5 after about 20 minutes. Now it turns east and descends once more through mature woods into a rocky valley. At the bottom, you cross a bridge over a stream that winds its way through a chaotic jumble of moss-covered rocks and fallen trees. The trail continues through rocky terrain along the bottom of a very large rock outcrop to a numberless post (which I presume to be Post 6) standing in a grove of hemlock and a little pocket of the relatively rare red spruce.

After a short ascent you emerge at the top of another cliff. This is more or less the halfway point of the loop. A welcome breeze wafts over the edge, and large flat rocks topped with red, white and jack pines make this a very pleasant place for lunch.

From the cliff, the trail makes a brief descent into yet another damp, rocky moss- and fern-clad hollow, and then climbs again to a third cliff, topped by huge flat rocks. At Post 7 there is a most beautiful jack pine at the very edge and, slightly further back, a very large boulder that looks like a piece of cubist sculpture.

After Post 7 the trail starts to slope downward toward Cloud Lake. A boardwalk makes it easy for you to cross over wetland as you approach the lake. There is a hushed stillness down here: the water, like glass; the grass, sedges and bordering trees, motionless. Cloud Lake itself is beautiful. Opposite Post 8, a huge rock rises from the lake. Water lilies spread out over the surface of the water, and at the edge, on your side, you might find iris and pitcher plant growing alongside clumps of bog laurel, cranberry and young tamarack.

You leave the boggy lakeside by climbing over a very large whale-backed rock. The trail then takes you through woods for about 700 metres until it reaches an intersection. Here you have the option of heading south toward Coon Lake if you wish. To stay on the main loop, turn right.

The main trail heads north over undulating terrain. After about ten minutes, you'll find yourself walking through trees, slightly above a boggy area. You then descend toward Post 9, with the boggy area on your left, and when you reach the pond you'll again notice signs of beaver activity. There is less shade here, and on a sunny day this stretch feels quite hot and exposed. The uneven terrain continues; the path at this point is quite rocky and interlaced with tree roots so you need to take care. After a few minutes you encounter a large meadow and pond on your left. The rocky path takes you to a little lookout over the pond and then back into trees once more.

Now you start the final ascent. You're walking through shade and suddenly the path underfoot is much softer. A short, sharp climb and you arrive, puffing and panting, at Post 10, which I think gives the best view of all, from a vantage point right above Whitefish Lake.

You reach Post 11 after a short five-minute walk along the cliff edge, enjoying wonderful panoramic views all the way. Soon the path starts to descend through the woods once more, and after about ten minutes, it brings you to a large and very beautiful beaver pond with still, clear waters. Multi-hued rocks line the edge, their pink, grey and green tints perfectly reflected in the lake's surface. Willow herb, yarrow, fern and steeple bush decorate the shoreline, and a small rocky island, with a huge pine surrounded by low shrubs, adds the final touch to a perfect picture. When you get to the end of the lake, you'll not be surprised to find an enormous beaver dam.

The trail turns left to begin its final descent toward the trailhead. After about ten minutes, you reach the point where the trail first diverged, and in another ten minutes, you are in the parking lot, tired, but I hope well pleased with your accomplishment.

Track and Tower Trail

This is a wonderful walk to do if your group has more than one car. At 13.2 km in length, it is the longest hike, but it's well worth the effort. If you enjoy walking through rapidly changing landscapes, this walk will not disappoint you. High cliffs, a narrow gorge, rapids, beautiful hardwood forest, wetland and a waterfall are just some of its contrasting natural features. The trail is replete with history, too; the remains of dams and log chutes, railway trestles and bridges serve as eloquent echoes and reminders of Algonquin's not-too-distant industrial past.

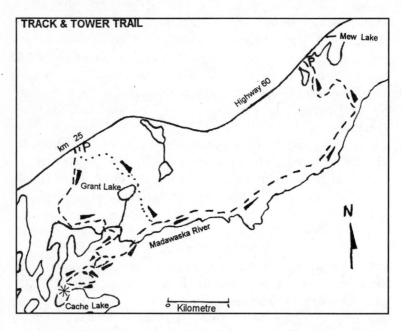

If you have only one car, don't be put off. The shorter trail, a 7.7-km loop gives you both the challenge of steep ascents and the reward of magnificent views. It also leaves you time to swim at one of the beach areas.

If you choose the long trek, leave one car at the Highland Trail parking area at km 29.7, and drive the other to the parking area for the Track and Tower Trail at km 25. Here you will see two trails. Take the one on the right. (The other is the returning trail for the loop.) For the first kilometre or so, you walk through a mature hardwood forest. Sometimes sunlight glints through the trees, but at ground level, the air feels cool and fresh under the shade of the high canopy. You get your first view of Cache Lake after about 20 minutes.

An eastbound train at Algonquin Park station.
Source: Algonquin Park Museum Archives #1634, National Film Board,
National Archives of Canada.

From Post 2, right at the edge of the lake, there is a splendid view of the trestles that used to carry the tracks of J.R. Booth's Ottawa, Arnprior and Parry Sound Railway. The railway brought many thousands of visitors to the park, and of the several lodges that were built to cater to their needs, the largest and the grandest was Highland Inn, which stood on the shore of Cache Lake, about 2 kilometres west of here. By 1910, it had accommodation for 150 people, a billiard room, tennis courts and a bowling green.

Its popularity lasted until the 1930s. After that, the advent of the highway, and an accompanying shift of public taste away from the grandiose and imposing, precipitated a decline for both hotel and railway. Nonetheless, when you look out over the water, it is not difficult to imagine the scene inside the passenger coaches during the inn's heyday, as the train trundled over the trestles, nearing its destination—children's excited shrieks, parental admonishments, hasty smoothing of skirts, donning of hats and feverish counting of boxes and suitcases.

Leaving Post 2, the trail follows the lake for a little way before entering mixed woods. You pass some impressively tall pines and

Algonquin Provincial Park

splendid yellow birch. As the path turns away from the lake, the trees become taller, and the ground is strewn with rocks and fallen trees. The forest thins out after a few minutes, making way for rich, ferny undergrowth and patches of grass. After about 15 minutes, the path reaches, then turns to follow, the Madawaska River.

At Post 3 you can walk onto the dam that stabilizes water levels between Cache Lake and the river. The present-day dam is thought to be very near the site of a wooden dam and logging chute, probably built during the 1880s to flush logs down river in steep, rocky places. You get an idea of what the scene might have been like if you stop just beyond the present dam, at a point where the trail crosses the river in an extremely narrow and rocky gorge. Some remains of the old wooden chute can still be seen strewn over the rocks as you pass through the gorge.

After three or four minutes, the gorge ends at a lovely water meadow where cattails, pickerel weed and Joe-pye weed thrive. For the next 300 metres or so, the trail follows the river, which alternates between stretches of calm water and small rapids. When the trail turns right, away from the river, you start to climb through beautiful woods. The climb becomes quite steep and the terrain rocky.

Be careful, at Post 5, to take the right-hand (ascending) path. It continues to climb through very tall trees past a huge rock face on your left. A jumble of talus covered with mosses and ferns lies at the foot of the cliff. When the path turns toward the cliff, it's quite a relief to find a wooden staircase to help you part of the way up. Then, you are on your own! The climb is quite steep, but short and only difficult in wet or freezing weather.

At the top, keep left. The path passes the site of an old fire tower, and a couple of minutes further on you come out onto a broad rock shelf overlooking Cache Lake. Even if there are other people on the cliff top, and usually there are (this is a very popular trail), you will forget them as soon as you turn to the utterly tranquil scene spread out before you. Cache Lake, with its deeply indented, thickly forested shoreline and small islands, is exceptionally beautiful. Not even the railway trestles are visible from here. The only sign of human presence is the occasional canoe gliding over the surface.

When you reach Post 8, stop for a moment and look northwest toward the Cache Lake parking area. This is where the grand old Highland Inn used to stand. A red pine plantation covers the ground now, but if you are curious, you might enjoy a visit to the site. (From the Cache Lake parking area a path goes through the

Ladies on the verandah of Highland Inn, ca 1910.
Source: Algonquin Park Museum Archives # 2853, Mary (Colson) Clare

plantation and along the railway platform that used to stand in front of the hotel. Some stairs leading from the train station to the inn still remain.)

From Post 8, the trail takes you back down the cliff, by way of the stairs. This time, when the path divides, take the right-hand trail, which descends to Post 9. Now you are walking along a level, somewhat elevated, wooded pathway with a rock face on your right. This is the bed of the Ottawa, Arnprior and Parry Sound railway and, if you are doing the long trail, you will be following it for the next 5.5 kilometres.

As you walk along, you appreciate the immensity of the task that faced the railway builders: rock faces to be cut through with dynamite; high embankments to be built with shovels; and rivers and waterways to be bridged with wooden trestles.

A couple of hundred metres along the railbed, you come to a crossing of the Madawaska. Beside Post 10 are the concrete foundations of a long steel trestle, built in 1899, at a height of 15 metres above the river, to carry the trains over a 110-metre gap to the other side of the valley. You appreciate just what a feat of engineering it was after you have scrambled down one side of the valley, crossed the river, and climbed up the other side.

If you are doing the loop, turn left at Post 11. An undulating trail will take you 2.5 kilometres, through a wooded landscape, past a very pretty lake at Post 12, and back to the parking area. If you are hiking the longer route, continue along the railbed. And if you think this sounds boring, think again!

After Post 13, the landscape opens out so that you find yourself walking along a high embankment in the middle of the wide water meadows adjacent to the river. (As this section is quite long, with no shade, be sure to keep plenty of drinking water handy.) Away over on your right, turkey vultures wheel over the top of huge cliffs that mark the edge of the river valley, and somewhere in the middle of the wetland, quite often hidden from view, the Madawaska wends its lazy way. As you walk along, the river curves in and out of sight; sometimes only the glimpse of the top of a canoeist's paddle, two arms and a head, tells you where it is; sometimes the trail passes along its bank. Wildflowers grow in profusion in this sunny place; in July, water lilies carpet the shallows, and virgin's bower clematis runs rampant over everything on the path. Keep an eye open for wildlife, too, along this stretch.

After about 3 kilometres, the wide, flat landscape ends. You leave the water meadows behind when the river picks up speed to run over rapids through a rocky gorge and into a pretty pool. Nearby, at Post 15, the trail turns away from the river and leaves the railbed. It climbs slowly but steadily to a ridge where there is a nice look-out to the south, over the valley. You are back into tree cover now, birch and spruce predominating.

When you come to an intersection, turn left for the final 1.8-kilometre trek along the Highland Backpacking Trail. But, if you have time to stop, before you start the last leg, walk a little way down the right-hand path. It brings you to a delightful waterfall where you can rest on the rocks and cool off. After the relative solitude of the last few hours you might find it a bit crowded—it's a very popular spot—but it's so scenic that it would be a pity to miss it. Anyhow the rest will set you up for the way home.

Back on the trail you ascend large rock slabs to the top of a peak overlooking Mew Lake. This last part is quite rugged, with many small ascents and descents and little level walking. The path is quite rocky, too, and strewn with tree roots, but the woods are beautiful. As you make your final descent to the parking area, you are bound to feel a great glow of accomplishment.

Booth's Rock Trail

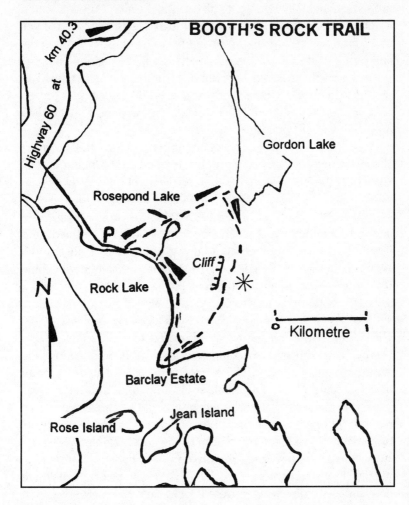

The 5.1-km Booth's Rock Trail is an excellent hike. In addition to offering some spectacular scenery, it takes you on an exploration of what used to be the private estate of Algonquin's most highly visible figure, lumber baron and railway builder J.R. Booth. Starting and finishing on the shores of Rock Lake, you walk through a wooded landscape to a splendid lookout, then descend to the lakeside to return to the starting point.

In 1895, as work started on the Ottawa, Arnprior and Parry Sound Railway, Booth bought a large tract of land on the west side of Rock Lake and two of the lake's three islands. On a promontory, he built a "cottage," which he gave to his daughter, Mrs. Gertrude Fleck. The Flecks named islands and lakes after their three children, Rose,

Algonquin Provincial Park

Gordon and Jean. Jean married Mr. Justice George Barclay, and the property eventually passed to them and became known as the Barclay Estate. The trail takes you through the estate, over the site of the farm, which probably supplied the main house with produce, and past the lakes and islands named after Booth's grandchildren.

This is a splendid walk on a hot day. For the first half of the hike, the thick forest gives cool shade and even if the heat gets to you after your stiff climb up Booth's Rock, plenty of spots for a cooling dip await you at Rock Lake.

Take the road to Rock Lake Campground at km 40.3. Turn left at the campground and drive one kilometre to the parking area. From here the trail leads left into trees. The ground is fairly level, if a little rocky underfoot, as you head east. For the first kilometre or so, the forest cover is thick, with hemlock predominating. After about 15 minutes, you reach tiny Rosepond Lake, named after Rose Fleck. Take a moment to go down to the water's edge. On a sunny, calm day, it is particularly striking; its shimmering blue waters present a vivid and brilliant contrast to the sombre black spruce trees that ring its shores.

Near Post 4 you'll notice that the thick forest-cover opens a little. This is the site of the farm that belonged to the Barclay Estate. Nature has taken over so completely that it's difficult to imagine anything being cultivated here. However, according to the trail booklet, cattle grazed, vegetable crops grew and an orchard was planted nearer to the lake. These few semi-cleared areas are all that remain. (Just past Post 4, don't be confused by a trail that appears to veer left; it just takes you to one of the cleared areas.)

At Post 5, the trail turns sharply right and starts to climb, quite steeply, through tall trees. It is rocky underfoot, so be careful if you're here on a wet day. Moss-covered rocks lie all around. The main ascent is accomplished by the time you reach Post 6, which stands in a magnificent grove of hemlocks. After this, you pass over undulating terrain for a few minutes before emerging at Post 7 on a broad rock shelf, 120 metres above Rock Lake. This is another magnificent view.

Directly below, the hardwood canopy, studded with taller, darker conifers, stretches to the lake. To your right, you can see the clear area where you began your walk and, in the distance, the southern end of Whitefish Lake. The land on the opposite shore rises steeply, to a height of 540 metres above sea level, and here and there, you get a glimpse of a rock face. The two steep, rocky hills on each side of the lake so impressed John Snow, who gave the lake its pertinent name, Rock Lake, that he described the west side as "rock perpendicular," and the cliff on which you are standing as "perpendicular mountain 500 ft." when he surveyed the land in 1854.

The trail follows the cliff face south, taking you past junipers, pines and cedars that somehow manage to survive without any visible nourishment. At Post 8, a leaning hemlock shows how precarious the hold of the vegetation is on the cliff edge.

Continuing south, you start to descend the cliff. A wooden staircase makes the going easier, and within 15 minutes you should be on the level ground at Post 9, close to the water. If you take the path straight ahead you can visit the remains of the Barclay Estate.

Until 1944, trains used to stop here to drop off or pick up guests. The path takes you along what must have once been a driveway lined with trees. You will appreciate that the small promontory would have been a wonderful site for a house—looking out on three sides over water, into beautiful forest on the fourth. What flowers you see depends, obviously, on the time of year you are there, but I have seen quite a show of asters and marguerites in the late summer. The many lilac trees must make quite a show earlier in the year. The tarmac tennis court—now sprouting weeds—is the most obvious survivor of the man-made structures. Down by the water, remnants of a dock remain, and offshore to your left are three islands. The two closest to the west shore are the ones named after Jean and Rose Fleck.

Retrace your steps to Post 9 and turn left onto the railbed, which hugs the east shore of the lake. The journey back to your starting point takes you through a narrow rock cut, along a high embankment and alongside wetland. If you are ready for a rest and a swim, now is your chance. There are some lovely spots along the shoreline, just north of the Barclay Estate. Hidden from the trail by trees and shrubs, large flat rocks at the water's edge give you smooth and easy entry into the cool water and a quiet, secluded place to stretch out after your swim. All in all, a very satisfying way to end a hike.

Other Algonquin Area Trails

Ragged Falls

The two trails mentioned in this section are outside Algonquin Park but each is so intimately connected with the park that it would be inappropriate to include them anywhere but here.

On Highway 60, immediately west of Algonquin Park and just east of Oxtongue Lake, there is a sign to a small park—Oxtongue

River–Ragged Falls Provincial Park. When you are hurrying to Algonquin, it's easy to ignore. Take my advice and have a look. It won't take long and you won't be disappointed.

The entrance road leads to a parking area. From there, a short trail heads through tall pines, hemlocks, and hardwood trees to Ragged Falls. Here, the Oxtongue River makes a wild and dramatic 25-metre plunge down a rocky chasm. You would think that you were miles away from anywhere—downed trees and fractured rock make a rough, chaotic scene. It's an impressive sight at any time of the year, but if you are lucky enough to catch the river during the spring freshet, when it puts on a truly dramatic display of roaring, raging power, you will be spellbound. However, from the viewing area, be prepared to receive quite a drenching! The fall is another good time to visit. There is less water, of course, but spectacular colour provides a drama of a different kind. What is more, at a time when Algonquin is overloaded with sightseers, at Ragged Falls, solitude can be almost guaranteed.

The Seguin Trail

If you have hiked either the Track and Tower or Booth's Rock Trail, you have already become acquainted with the remains of the Arnprior, Ottawa and Parry Sound Railway. Toward the line's western end, between Highways 69 and 11, a 61-kilometre stretch of the rail bed has been made into a recreational trail. The Seguin Trail offers an opportunity not only to hike through the countryside along the railway's route but also to explore some of the adjacent

Blasting rock during the construction of the OA & PS railway.
Source: Algonquin Park Museum Archives # 123, J. W. Ross

Clearing a cut on the OA & PS railway, 1894.
Source: Algonquin Park Museum Archives # 156, J. W. Ross

communities, bustling and prosperous during the railway's heyday, now silent and deserted.

The Seguin Trail is not difficult; however, exploring it is easier if your group has two cars. There are several points of access along Highway 518, where you can park one car, then drive to the next. Shirley Teasdale, in *Hiking Ontario's Heartland*, recommends a 13-kilometre section, running between Orville and Seguin Falls and a 16-kilometre section running between Highway 69 and the little hamlet of Swords.

If you like to camp, Algonquin Park has eight campgrounds for you to choose from along the Highway 60 Corridor. Services vary but, overall, the campgrounds on Coon Lake and Tea Lake are the least developed. If you are not a camper you will find a large and varied selection of accommodation both west and east of the Park boundary.

There are three lodges within the park: Arowhon Pines, on Little Joe Lake (705) 633-5661, Bartlett Lodge, on Cache Lake (705) 633-5543, and Killarney Lodge, on Lake of Two Rivers (705) 633-5551. I have stayed at just one, so I can comment only on Killarney Lodge. It is ideally placed for all the hikes and even though it's right on Highway 60 it's amazingly quiet. If you get a cabin facing across the lake you feel very secluded. I can recommend it unreservedly —if it's your idea of heaven to return from a challenging hike to good food and very comfortable digs, this is the place.

A wide variety of accommodation is to be found just outside the park. See page 149 for useful contact numbers.

Georgian Bay's Eastern Shore

Samuel de Champlain was the first European to leave a written description of Georgian Bay. In 1615, he journeyed by canoe from Quebec to Huronia via the Ottawa River, Lake Nipissing and the French River. When he reached the open waters of Georgian Bay, he was mightily impressed by its size—he instantly named it the Freshwater Sea—and by the abundance and variety of its fish. He commented on the "great number of islands," and noted that shore itself was "partly rugged, partly flat, uninhabited by savages and slightly covered by trees, including oaks."

Champlain's route took him south through the archipelago, across the Severn Sound to a Huron village called Otouacaha, probably on the tip of the peninsula at Thunder Bay in Tiny Township. There, he was agreeably surprised to find a region of rolling hills, well fed by streams, and a fine crop of corn growing on cultivated land. It was, he wrote, "very pleasant, in contrast to such a bad country as that through which we had just come."

Today, a canoeist paddling southward along the east shore of Georgian Bay would find many changes—some bustling communities and numerous boats plying the waters—but Champlain's landscape is still recognizable. Much of the wave-washed, rocky shoreline looks as daunting and inhospitable as ever. The crucial difference, of course, is the thousands of cottages that sit on the islands of the archipelago. These are ever-present reminders that the very things that for centuries made settlement so difficult— remoteness, inaccessibility and bare, windswept rock—have become prized ingredients to the twentieth-century town-dweller looking for the ideal wilderness retreat.

On approaching the Penetang Peninsula, today's canoeist will find, like Champlain before him, that the landscape undergoes a change. Rocky islands and low-lying barren shores give way to boulder and sand beaches topped by high, tree-covered bluffs with rolling countryside behind. The sudden change in topography is due to geology. Somewhere in the middle of the Severn Sound is the edge of the Canadian Shield, and on the Penetanguishene Peninsula the Precambrian rocks of the Shield are overlain by a

Canoeing in the 30,000 Islands in 1837—Sketch by Anna Jameson.
Source: Archives of Ontario, Acc 2305 S-4297

layer of sedimentary rock. This softer bedrock, which yielded much more readily to the brutal onslaught of glaciers and the relentless buffeting of post-glacial waves, has been moulded into a much more benign, gently rolling landscape. Here, deeper soils made it suitable for agriculture and, therefore, much more conducive to human settlement.

Indeed, compared with the Shield lands immediately to the north, where no permanent settlement took place until well into the nineteenth century, the Penetanguishene Peninsula has a long and fascinating human history.

The Hurons were the first settlers; they adapted to agriculture around A.D. 1100 and, more than 500 years ago, were leading a relatively settled existence on the Penetanguishene Peninsula, living in villages and raising corn, beans and squash. Europeans didn't enter the picture until the seventeenth century, and even then their stay was short. Jesuit missionaries set up camp at Sainte-Marie and for 20 years ministered to the surrounding Huron villages. But, in 1648, Iroquois from the south attacked the Hurons and the following year murdered some of the Jesuits. In the wake of the massacre, the missionaries and a few Huron survivors retreated to St. Joseph's (now Christian) Island; however, after a winter of starvation and further Iroquois attack, the missionaries packed up and returned to Quebec.

Even when the soil was suitable for agriculture, getting rid of the stumps was no easy matter. A stumping bee in Simcoe County in 1882.
Source: Archives of Ontario, Acc 3062 S-7849

One hundred and fifty years were to elapse before the Europeans returned. First to arrive, was the British navy—by 1820, twenty naval vessels were maintained at the naval base at Penetanguishene. Then, around 1840, with the influx of the first of many waves of European immigrants, the peninsula embarked on a period of growth and boom—centred predictably on the logging industry—that was to last well into the twentieth century.

Northwards along the Georgian Bay shore, the story of settlement is very different. Here, on the islands and along the heavily indented shoreline, the rocky lands were unsuitable for settlement. A report on the lands around the Moon River, submitted in 1861 by surveyor John Stoughton Dennis, noted, "The country...is very much broken and is so rocky and swampy...as to afford little or no land fit for farming purposes." Of course some hardy souls did eke out a living, but the few settlements that did grow up were very firmly tied to logging operations. Depot Harbour, for example, the company town built by lumber magnate J.R. Booth at the terminus of his railway, the Ottawa, Arnprior and Parry Sound Railway, once had more than 3,000 residents. However, the town of Parry Sound is the only sizable community that survives today.

There are some wonderful hikes along the Georgian Bay shore-line. Fortunately, the presence of one national and three provincial parks gives some assurance that private ownership will not appro-priate every last square metre of a spectacular and sometimes wild landscape. In the four parks, there are hikes ranging from easy to challenging that take you over rapidly changing and diverse terrain. Awenda Provincial Park, at the northern tip of the Penetanguishene Peninsula, and Killbear Provincial Park on the north shore of Parry Sound, with their drive-in campsites, and their diversity of recre-ational opportunities, organized programs and hikes, are perfect places for families. Georgian Bay National Park on Beausoleil Island and The Massasauga Provincial Park offer the chance to experi-ence the variety of terrains of the islands. And last, but not least, a very difficult and rugged trail along the shores of McCrae Lake tra-verses the truly wild country just east of the Georgian Bay shore. Without doubt, this is the toughest hike in the book; it's a wonderful challenge, but be warned—it is for fit and experienced hikers only.

Awenda Provincial Park

Awenda Provincial Park is the only area in this book that is not on the Canadian Shield, and its landscape is quite different from other places along the Georgian Bay shoreline. Unlike the parks on the Shield, with their large areas of exposed rock, in Awenda, a thick layer of glacial debris covers the bedrock. The park's most distinctive natural feature is a 32-metre bluff, formed 5,500 years ago by the action of the waves of Lake Nipissing—a larger ancestor of Lake Huron. The bluff is crowned by tall, mixed forest, and at its base, wide sand and cobble beaches stretch out into clear, shallow water.

Awenda's human history is no less interesting: seventeen archaeological sites have yielded evidence of four different cultures and 11,000 years of human activity; Etienne Brûlé, the young Frenchman sent by Champlain to live among the Hurons, is thought to have stayed hereabouts, perhaps even to have been killed here in 1633; and in the mid-nineteenth century, homesteaders settled here.

The park has 200 hundred large, sheltered, drive-in campsites. A wide range of programs, four beaches, and an inland lake make it a perfect place for families. Twenty-nine kilometres of hiking trails afford an opportunity to explore the park's diverse natural and cultural environment. The trails range in length from 1 to 13 kilometres. Each has its own character and none is difficult. They may be combined in many different ways, so the only real decision you have to make is how far you want to walk.

Georgian Bay's Eastern Shore

2

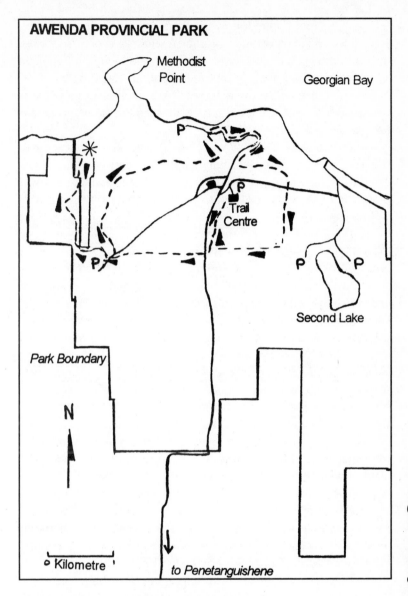

AWENDA PROVINCIAL PARK

Methodist
Point

Georgian Bay

Trail
Centre

Second Lake

Park Boundary

N

Kilometre

to Penetanguishene

Bluff, Dunes and Beach Loop

A fascinating and immensely varied walk of about 10.5 kilometres takes you from the Trail Centre south and east through woods, out over the dunes and back, then west along the edge of the bluff. The trail then makes a steep descent to the shore before climbing back up to follow the bluff back to the start. To get the best out of the many fine views along this trail, you should do the walk in early spring, before the trees are in leaf.

From the Trail Centre follow the Bluff–Brûlé trail signs, heading south through tall hardwoods forest on a wide, level path. In spring, the ground here is covered with trilliums. After about 800 metres, take the Brûlé Trail heading off to the right, first crossing the main park road. Once across the road you'll see pines among the hardwoods and, alongside the trillium, violets and foamflowers that are just about to bloom.

When you reach a second road, take the Dunes Trail, which will take you out toward the lake, along sand dunes created 11,000 years ago during the retreat of the ice. The trail starts a gentle ascent, still passing through tall mixed woods, which in spring are carpeted with yellow violets.

By the time the trail turns north, toward the lake, you have moved into a different environment—the landscape is much more open, and you can glimpse a long ridge to your left. The path is strewn with pine needles and at one point passes through a narrow corridor, bordered by staghorn sumac and scotch pine. Soon you'll encounter signs of an old farm, built in 1902 by the Newberry family. Where the trail veers to the left, you'll see stone foundations and, a couple of minutes along the trail, the remains of a house and some outbuildings. The area is dotted with apple trees, but large stands of staghorn sumac are now beginning to take over.

Beyond the farm, the path passes through undulating countryside with good, clear views on both sides. It passes briefly over privately owned land where the ground has been cleared and planted with Christmas trees, then it climbs up a steepish sand bank to a spectacular lookout over Georgian Bay. Beckwith, Hope and Christian Islands are on your left, and Giant's Tomb Island on your right.

You must retrace your steps from the lookout, but this is no hardship. You'll see quite different aspects of the landscape and, if the weather is clear, you'll get an excellent view over to the wooded ridge to the west. (The Dunes trail takes about an hour.)

Back at the road, head north (left) along Bluff Trail. There is a maze of trails as you pass Deer Campground, so keep a lookout for a sign that takes you off to the left, toward the edge of the bluff. After about 2.5 kilometres of very pleasant walking through the tall trees, you come to an intersection. Take the left fork, heading down the bluff. Shortly, you'll find yourself walking through a stand of very large beeches. In spring the ground underneath is carpeted with both red and white trilliums, interspersed with the lacy, delicate leaves and nodding heads of Dutchman's breeches.

By the time you reach the 155 steps that take you down the bluff, you have entered a much damper ecosystem. The landscape here is especially dramatic: hemlocks lend a dark, brooding presence, and among the trees lie enormous rocks cloaked in moss, ferns and shrubs. Look carefully and you may see jack-in-the-pulpit growing on the top of the biggest rock of all.

The trail brings you to the boardwalk by the lakeshore. Turn right to walk along First Beach. Its very peaceful and pretty—sand and smooth rocks, calm water and a perfect view of Giant's Tomb Island. From the northeast end of the beach, climb back up the bluff via the road. At the top, you can either return to the Trail Centre via the road (about 750 metres) or, if you feel like continuing through the woods for a while, turn left and continue east on the Bluff Trail. It takes you along the bluff edge and, if you are there before the trees are in full leaf, you'll get some lovely views over the water. After one kilometre, the trail veers south. About 200 metres further on, it crosses the park road. Stay on the Bluff Trail until it meets a gravel road, then turn right. After about one more kilometre you'll meet up with the Bluff Trail once again. Turn right and retrace your steps the 800 metres or so to the Trail Centre.

Beausoleil Island

Trail Information: On Beausoleil Island eleven trails form a 30-kilometre trail network. Each trail has a name, and the loops described below incorporate a number of different trails. At the north end of the island, each trail has it own coloured marker.

Southern Loop, Southbound—6.5-kilometre loop, 2–2.5 hours, moderate

Central Loop, Northbound—11-kilometre loop, 4–5 hours, moderate to strenuous

North Shore Loop—10.5-kilometre loop, 4–5 hours, moderate to strenuous

Access: From Highway 400, near Port Severn, take Muskoka Road 5 to Honey Harbour. Privately-owned water taxi services to Beausoleil Island operate from several marinas in Honey Harbour, from May to October.

Map: A free Visitors' Guide, which includes a map of the island and the hiking trails, is available from the Park Headquarters, opposite the General Store, in Honey Harbour. All park users must pay a fee.

Parking: At the Honey Harbour marinas.

Guarding the entrance to Severn Sound, Beausoleil Island is the largest of the 59 islands that make up the Georgian Bay Islands National Park. Although this island is only 8 kilometres long and 2 kilometres wide, its rocky shores and tranquil woodland offer the hiker a surprising range of hikes.

The clue to Beausoleil's variety lies in its position. Perched on the very edge of the Canadian Shield, it has two distinct personalities. At its northern end lies a ragged shoreline, indented by myriad small bays and inlets. The landscape is dominated by large outcrops of granite, adorned with stubby junipers and stunted, windswept pines. In contrast, at the southern end, where rock is covered by soil, stands a tall hardwood forest whose high canopy gives cool and airy shade even on the hottest days.

If you don't have a boat, don't worry. Water taxis take you from one of several marinas in Honey Harbour to wherever you choose to land. The journey, which is an adventure in itself, takes about 15 to 20 minutes, depending on traffic. If you're there on a weekend, the bay will be pretty busy with boats of all shapes and sizes (some of the more ostentatious ones tiered like wedding cakes) jockeying for their turn to make their way through the narrow lanes that lead to open water. Once you are through Big Dog Channel, the crowd

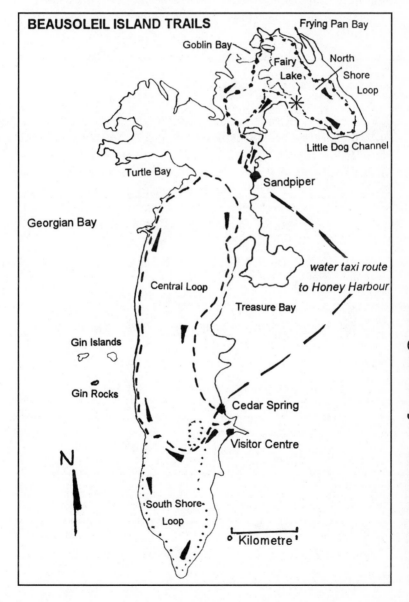

BEAUSOLEIL ISLAND TRAILS

Frying Pan Bay

Goblin Bay

Fairy Lake

North Shore Loop

Little Dog Channel

Turtle Bay

Sandpiper

Georgian Bay

water taxi route to Honey Harbour

Central Loop

Treasure Bay

Gin Islands

Gin Rocks

Cedar Spring

Visitor Centre

N

South Shore Loop

Kilometre

disperses and your taxi driver puts on a mighty spurt as he heads for the island.

Where you choose to land depends on what you want to do. You can't really cover all of the island in a day, so if your time is limited and you want a challenging hike, head for the north end. If you are able to stay overnight, you may as well head for the main drop-off point, Cedar Spring, which is close to the Visitor Centre, beaches, picnic area and the largest campground (the only one with flush toilets and showers). However long or short your stay, remember that you have to carry in everything that you need, apart from drinking water and firewood.

Southern and Central Loops

Before you start, call in at the Visitor Centre and view the slide show that tells you about the island's natural and human history. Then, follow signs to the Compound to visit the site of an Ojibwa village, settled between 1842 and 1858 by a band known as the Beausoleil Band. They fished for bass in nearby waters and cleared land to grow corn and potatoes. But it was a hard life. The soil quickly became exhausted, and they often had to clear land on neighbouring islands to grow enough food to subsist. The little Cemetery of the Oaks in a clearing to the left of the trail remains a poignant testament to the harshness of their existence and to the many—especially the very young—who died untimely deaths.

Both the South and Central Loops start out on Christian Trail. From the compound it takes you through a meadow to a viewpoint. Wildflowers enliven the scene throughout the season but bloom in great profusion in spring. In early June, bright yellow, deep blue and white intermingle as you walk past patches of pussytoes, St. John's wort, viper's bugloss and bladder campion. Later in the season, pink and blue predominate as the waving heads of bergamot and vervain compete for your attention.

Beyond the viewpoint, the trail veers right to cross the island. Soon you enter a tall beech and maple forest, which has an airy feel to it. After 100 metres or so, the Firetower Trail goes off to the right. It's a lovely detour, taking you through stands of very large old-growth trees, and if you are there in early spring the ground will be carpeted with trillium, trout lily and Canada mayflower.

Back on Christian Trail, you continue west along a level path. After about ten minutes you will notice thick clumps of balsam fir

A few families remained on Beausoleil Island until 1929.
Mrs. Mudwah and the Tobey children at the Tobey homestead
(now Cedar Springs Campground).
Source: Georgian Bay Islands National Park

and hemlock amidst the hardwoods and, if you stop and listen, you may hear the faint throbbing of the waves breaking on the windward shore. In a few more minutes, you emerge onto a boulder beach. Here, the island has a quite different feel to it. Exposed to the wind and waves, this shoreline has a much wilder, harsher mien.

Now you have a decision to make. Christian Trail ends at the beach, where it meets Georgian Trail. Until fairly recently, Georgian Trail followed the western shore all the way from Turtle Bay to Beausoleil Point. However, a severe spring storm two or three years ago caused such devastation that the stretch of trail running between Brébeuf Island and Christian Beach had to be closed.

Although the trail remains closed, when the lake water is low, it is possible to hike along the shore. When this is feasible, I recommend the route north. However, if water levels are too high and you must head south, a very pleasant hike of about 4.5 kilometres—mostly through forest—will take you along Georgian Trail to the southern tip of the island, then back to the compound, via Huron Trail.

If you are up for a much longer, more varied hike, and the water is low, turn right. Your route along the shore will be rugged, but it will have many compensations. The vast expanse's of sparking water and rugged shoreline are a delight to the eye; gulls and terns endlessly wheel and dive offshore, while at the water's edge sandpipers dart back and forth, following the path of each wave, never getting a foot wet.

After about 1.5 kilometres, you'll pass a little group of islands called Gin Islands and Rocks—rumoured to be a favourite picnic spot of Lady Simcoe—perhaps named after her tipple of choice? After a further 2 kilometres, just as you come up to Turtle Bay, you pass Brébeuf Island, named after the Jesuit martyr, Jean de Brébeuf. (Its lighthouse, still intact, was built in 1900.) On warm, sunny days, this is a good spot to catch a glimpse of turtles sunning themselves on the rocks.

When you reach Huron Trail, follow it as it makes a wide sweep in a southeasterly direction back across the island. After 30 thirty minutes, you emerge onto the tranquil, wooded shores of Treasure Bay. From here, an easy hour's walk brings you back to Cedar Spring. You have a choice: Huron Trail is the most direct route back to the compound, but I prefer to take Treasure Trail, which goes down to the edge of the bay and continues along the shoreline. Mallard, heron and kingfisher are just a few of the many residents of the shallow waters. And if you haven't yet had a swim, there is a long, sandy beach at Cedar Spring, where the water is calm and warm—a perfect way to end your day.

North Shore Loop

This hike is marginally shorter but, still strenuous. There are many rocks to clamber over and very few level stretches of trail, but the views from the high points are superb. If you have only one day, and you are in reasonable shape, choose the north end of the island.

The last time I did this walk, the water taxi dropped me at the Wana Keta picnic area. From there, a short trail takes you inland to

Massasauga Trail (purple markers). Turn right to head north. The path here is pretty level and takes you through a mixture of forest and wetland. After about 20 minutes, Portage Trail (white markers) goes off to the left to cross the island at its narrowest point. The crossing, which takes less than 15 minutes, takes you from wetland to an unequivocally Shield landscape of rounded, barren rocks, adorned only with lichens and great clumps of juniper. On the rocky terrain at the north end of the island, it is sometimes difficult to see just where the path is. If you are not sure where to head next, stand alongside the coloured trail marker and, if you look around carefully, you will spot the next one.

When Portage Trail ends, turn right onto the green-marked Rockview Trail. Now, the rocks are getting bigger and you are climbing to higher ground. After about ten minutes, you reach an area of very large, flat rocks. Here, Rockview Trail meets an orange-marked trail that circles round a lake. This is Fairy Trail, and here you turn left. After a few minutes you will get a view of Fairy Lake on your right. It's a beautiful sight with its calm waters, and well-treed, rocky shores. If you have your binoculars with you, you are almost certain to spot at least one pair of loons.

Fairy Trail soon veers to the right and starts a 15-minute descent to Goblin Bay. The bay is charming. There's a tiny beach and great rock shelf to sit on that catches the stiff breeze coming in off the water. From there you can watch opulent cruisers plying the open waters beyond the bay. It's a great place for a swim or a lunch break.

From Goblin Bay, Fairy Trail continues north. First, you climb a little to a fine viewpoint that overlooks a small lake on your right and Goblin Bay on your left. You pass a short trail that leads down to the campsites at tiny Honeymoon Bay. Shortly after, the trail enters woods and continues to descend through a rather swampy area. Still passing through trees, the trail gradually makes a turn around the northern edge of the island. About half an hour beyond Honeymoon Bay, the trail veers south, still in forest, but soon starts to climb. A little way along, just off the trail, there is a wonderful, high rocky outcrop that affords great views of Frying Pan Bay and the main channel beyond. It's another great stopping place, or, if you fancy going down to the water, a short scramble will take you to a breezy rock on the shores of the long narrows of Frying Pan Bay.

Back on the trail you continue south through woods for about 15 minutes. When you meet Cambrian Trail you have a choice: you can either continue on Fairy Trail for 20 minutes to complete the Fairy Lake circuit, or you can explore the northeast portion of the island on Cambrian Trail. If you have the energy for another hour of walking, take Cambrian Trail.

Cambrian Trail takes you east, then south, through woods. As you go south, the trees get bigger (and the mosquitoes get more plentiful), but if you're wearing your trusty bug shirt, you won't be too discommoded). After about 35 minutes, the trail comes to the shore of Little Dog Channel, the very narrow strip of water that separates Beausoleil Island from Little Beausoleil Island. The channel seems to be a favourite spot for small boats, and it's a bit of a shock to see a cottage only a few metres away. But the intrusion of civilization does not last long; the trail soon turns away from the water and starts to climb again. As you leave the trees behind, the path becomes rockier and a breeze springs up. This ascent takes you to what is probably the most spectacular point on the island. Where Cambrian Trail meets up again with Fairy Trail, there is a high, rocky spot with great views both north and south. To the north, Fairy Lake lies still, tranquil and deserted; to the south, Beausoleil Bay hums with a continuous, colourful bustle of boats.

Follow Fairy Trail west for about 10 minutes, then turn left onto Massasauga Trail. Rock gradually gives way to forest as you head south. After about half an hour, you'll reach your original point of departure. All you have to do now is to retrace your steps, and in about 25 minutes, you'll be back at the Wana Keta area and you can laze on the rocks while you wait for your taxi.

McCrae Lake Nature Reserve

Trail Information: McCrae Lake Trail—8-kilometre linear trail (16 kilometres in all), 7 hours, strenuous. Or 2.5-kilometre linear trail (5 kilometres in all), 2 hours, moderate.

Access: From Highway 400, north of Port Severn and about 6.5 kilometres north of District Road 34, turn onto Georgian Bay Road. After you have passed underneath the Highway, turn right, onto the ramp leading up to southbound Highway 69. A few metres along the ramp, a slip road leads left, down a hill to a car park.

Map: A topographical map of the Gibson Trail System, a wilderness area maintained by the Five Winds Ski Touring Club, is available from the club. This map is essential if you are going to attempt any of the Five Winds trails. Contact the Five Winds Membership Secretary, 18 Randolph Road, Toronto, ON M4G 3R7, or call (416) 635-2702.

Parking: At McCrae Lake parking area.

McCrae Lake Nature Reserve is a wilderness area a few kilometres north of Beausoleil Island. Just west of Highway 69, a large and irregularly shaped lake lies hidden among thickly wooded, rolling hills. Along its shores, pine and juniper maintain a precarious hold on the towering outcrops of gneiss and granite that rise steeply from its waters. Of course, the large stands of white pine that once dominated its forests are long gone—victims of the frenzied logging of the mid-1800s. Today, a new forest flourishes, and in the hollows, where rock gives way to soil, dark stands of hemlock, spruce and pine, and graceful, mature, mixed hardwoods have obliterated the old scars.

A rocky strip of land at the lake's western end all but separates it from Georgian Bay. The channel through which the lake drains is so narrow that access by anything larger than a canoe is well-nigh impossible. This fortuitous quirk of geography has saved the lake from development, and not a single cottage stands on its shores. For the hiker who loves wildness and solitude and savours the

Georgian Bay's Eastern Shore

4

challenge of a rocky, rugged and sometimes elusive trail, McCrae Lake is a wonderful place to explore. Here you can stand alone on a rocky shelf high above the blue waters and be sure that the silence and tranquility will be broken only by the sudden flash of a great blue heron, the call of a loon, or the hypnotic, rhythmic progress of a lone canoe.

But make no mistake: this is not an area for the novice hiker. The trail is one of several marked but ungroomed wilderness trails maintained by the Five Winds Ski Touring Club. From the car park to the end of the lake is a distance of about 8 kilometres. The journey will take the best part of three hours each way, and once you are on the trail, there is no other access by road. There is no flat ground, most of the time the going is rough and rugged, the trail marked only by small cairns and infrequent blazes. If you plan to do the full hike, the map provided by the Five Winds Ski Touring Club and a compass are essential pieces of equipment. However, if you suspect that you are not sufficiently experienced for the long haul, don't despair, there is a shorter option. The first 2.5 kilometres of the trail—an hours hike along a well-blazed path over undulating terrain—leads to a high, rocky outcrop overlooking the lake. From here, there is easy access to the lakeside and good swimming, which makes this a very satisfying half-day outing, particularly in hot weather. But if you are fit and experienced and can use a compass, do the whole hike. You won't regret it.

McCrae Lake Trail

At the car park, turn your back on the notice board and walk south for about 15 metres. The path, marked by yellow plastic rectangles, goes off to your right, ascending through scrub which rapidly becomes shady, mixed bush with ferny undergrowth. After about ten minutes, you will come across a log path to take you across a marshy area. You soon begin to ascend over rockier ground carpeted with junipers, and after another ten minutes the path reaches an open area where staghorn sumacs grow among flat-topped rocks.

Another ten minutes further along, the trail descends into a damper environment dominated by tall, mixed hardwoods. Logs again take you over the wet remnants of a stream bed, then the trail begins to ascend once more. If you are here in the spring, look out for lady's slipper orchids. Soon you get your first glimpse of water,

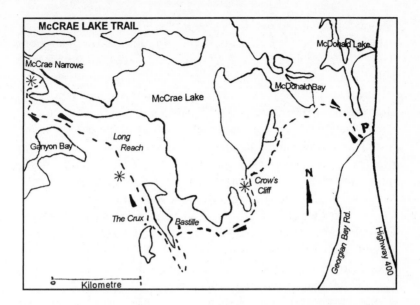

McCrae Narrows

McDonald Lake

McDonald Bay

McCrae Lake

P

Long Reach

Ganyon Bay

Crow's Cliff

N

The Crux

Bastille

Georgian Bay Rd.

Highway 400

0   Kilometre   1

and through the trees you can see a small rocky island just off the shore of McDonald Bay. The path follows the rather wet shoreline, crosses more marshy ground (in spring, the route is lined with bunchberry), then moves away from the shore.

The trail starts to climb again ten minutes later to higher, drier ground, skirting around large rocks clad with lichens and junipers, and dotted with stands of staghorn sumac. Another descent brings you into beautiful, airy, mature hardwoods, and for a while the path takes an easy, undulating course beneath the high, shady canopy. But not for long. A short, steep ascent carries you out of the tall trees and brings you onto a dramatic, rocky outcrop, called Crow's Cliff, high above McCrae Lake.

Pines and cedars cling to the edge, and large carpets of juniper bushes fill the cracks and hollows. Walk toward the edge and you'll come to a wonderful lookout on top of a rounded rock. There is a wide ledge just below, so don't panic. The view over the south arm of the lake is spectacular. To the north a large island guards the entrance to the south arm; on either side, narrow channels lead out to the main body of the lake. Beyond the island's rocky shoreline, ridge after ridge of wooded hills rises up, stretching to the horizon— dramatic at any time, but if you happen to be there in the fall, a glorious sight. The lake itself will be deserted except, perhaps, for the flash of a great blue heron.

Directly below, where a rocky promontory intrudes into the lake, there are wonderful places to swim and laze on the rocks.

Georgian Bay's Eastern Shore

They are not hard to get to. A little further along the trail a steep path leads down to the flat rocks that line the narrow inlet. For those who are not up for the long haul this is a wonderful stopping place. But if you are going the distance, don't linger too long.

The path follows the rocky edge in a southerly direction, and after about three minutes passes the steep path descending on the right toward the lake. The main trail, however, continues south, at first picking its way through juniper-clad rocks, then making a short descent into woods. After a minute or two, it climbs once more onto drier, rocky ground, skirts round the end of the narrow inlet, then begins to head in a westerly direction. You need to keep a sharp lookout for blazes in this area. There is no visible trail through the rocks, simply a succession of blazes interspersed by a few cairns. As you reach each one, look for the next; it should be visible. If you walk for more than a minute without sighting a blaze or a cairn, be careful; you may have wandered off the route.

Keep an eye open for a sharpish right turn, which takes you down into woods, about one kilometre (20 minutes) past the look-out. After the turn, you get a brief glimpse of the southernmost tip of McCrae Lake on the right, then the path enters a dark grove of hemlock, taking you over a stream. After a few minutes, it skirts left round a very large rock, traverses more flat rocks, veers to the left again and soon plunges into tall hemlocks. A few minutes later, the path starts to rise steeply, skirting around the base of a very large rock, aptly called The Bastille. A sharp left turn near the top brings you back onto rocks and more open terrain.

Marked largely by cairns, the route heads south for about 400 metres, picking its way through very large, flat rocks, many of them coloured with alternating bands of pink and grey. When you reach a point where the trail veers slightly to the right to pass briefly through a stand of hemlocks, be particularly watchful. The trail brings you out of the hemlocks and up a steep rock. At the top there is a cairn. Close by, you will see two blazes placed sideways, one above the other, on a small oak tree. Here, the trail makes a very sharp right turn, almost doubling back on itself. At the turn you will see a cairn down to your right and another blaze on a tree. A couple of minutes later, when there appears to be a choice of paths, keep to the right and head north over a large flat rock toward a blaze on a tree.

The blazes in this area are not easy to follow but if you are vigilant you'll be all right. After about 15 minutes, you should see water straight ahead, and you'll shortly reach a very large beaver pond. The trail brings you to a fine lookout (on the map it's labelled The Crux) above the pond. You are now just past the halfway point of the outward journey. On a hot day you'll probably encounter a welcome breeze so it's a good place for a short rest and a drink.

From the lookout, the path veers first right, then left, to follow the water's edge. It crosses a small spit of land between two ponds, skirting round the bottom of a very large rock that is on your left side. Again, spotting the blazes can be difficult, but it's not impossible. Soon you'll pass a cairn on a rock and a blaze on a nearby tree and ascend once more into open country.

You are now in an area known as Long Reach and, for the next half hour, you will hop from cairn to cairn over rough, rocky ground where juniper, small oak and pine maintain a stubborn hold in inhospitable surroundings. The path ascends slowly but steadily, taking you on a wide curve, moving gradually round to head west. After about ten minutes, you will notice a cottage on your left and a few minutes later, as you pass a second, green-roofed cottage, the waters and curved shoreline of Ganyon Bay come into view ahead. It's at this point that you appreciate your ascent. The high plateau where you stand gives long, wonderful views in every direction. High, wooded ridges rise to the north and east; to your left, the huge whale-backed rocks lining the shores of Ganyon Bay seem very close. You'll likely see boats plying its waters, for the bay, unlike McCrae Lake, is accessible to traffic.

Another ten minutes of cairn hopping brings you to the sight of water on your right—a reassuring sign that you are not too far from the end of McCrae Lake. In fact, you are on a narrow spit of land, no wider than 250 metres, which runs between Ganyon Bay and the westernmost arm of the lake. Cairns and blazes are a bit sparse here, so it's best to keep heading rightish toward McCrae Lake— the trail passes within about 30 metres of the shore. If you are in doubt, about five minutes after McCrae Lake comes into view, look for an enormous rock (an erratic, part of the glacial legacy, I suspect) and you'll find the trail to its right. After five more minutes the trail starts to descend, leaving the rocks and entering mixed forest once more. As you near the water's edge, the trail veers left to skirt round the edge of the last bay. The path here is quite overgrown, but look carefully and you'll see the blazes.

Once round the bay, the trail makes a steep ascent to a rocky outcrop. Look right and you'll see a rock with a splotch of yellow, and a blaze on a small oak tree nearby. From here you are just steps from a splendid high vantage point giving marvellous views

This area of Georgian Bay was not always so peaceful. During its heyday, ca 1900, Muskoka Mills, at the mouth of the Musquash River, employed 82 workers and produced 8,500,000 feet of lumber a season.
Source: Archives of Ontario, Acc 13688-4

over the end of the lake and McCrae Narrows, the tiny channel that connects the lake to Georgian Bay. At this point you will have been on the trail for three hours and you will be more than ready for a rest, and if it's hot, a swim.

It's not difficult to get down to the water. Down to your right you'll see some very large flat rocks at the water's edge. Retrace your steps to the blazed oak tree and you'll find that the blazes do actually direct you down the hill from the tree, bringing you to the rocky shore at a tranquil spot where large rocks give access to deep water—the perfect spot not only for lunch but also for a swim.

It's also possible to get down to very end of the lake. From the blazed oak tree, a very steep, rough trail leads down to the narrowest part of the channel—a gap of only a few feet. Even though it is very tempting, I have never made it across the divide to some wonderfully inviting flat rocks on the other side. Each time I have been about to try, I have been intimidated by the speed of the water and by visions of my hiking boots making their escape mid-stream and floating merrily out to Georgian Bay. It would be a long way back barefoot!

Have a good rest but do be careful not to lose track of the time; remember that the return journey will also take up to three hours, maybe longer, because trail markers seem to be even less frequent on the return leg. When you are ready for the homeward journey, find your way to the rock with the yellow splotch. About 30 metres past it, you'll see the path descending to your left. It's easy to miss, so take care. And as you go round the bay, be careful to keep a sharp lookout for a right turn, marked by a blaze on an oak tree, which takes you up a hill toward the high plateau.

Cairns and blazes are not plentiful across this open plateau. It is best to go right up to to each cairn or blaze, then to look for the next marker. Each time I have done the walk, I've lost sight of the trail a couple of times (but never twice in the same place). When I was really stumped I found it helpful to locate blazes pointing in the outbound direction, then to hunt for the elusive return markers. However, having said that, I don't want to give the impression that the return journey is tiresome. It isn't. There are many fine views and some totally new perspectives. For example, the panorama to the south over Ganyon Bay and the hills behind is particularly dramatic.

The only really difficult moment on the return journey occurs shortly after the halfway point. Here you approach a crucial turn sign that signals the trail's very abrupt change of direction from south to north. You will approach the spot about 20 to 25 minutes (about 500 metres) after you have left the rocky lookout over the beaver pond. The trail passes over large, flattish rocks, through a very open area, and brings you toward two cairns, one on your left, one on your right. Near the cairns is a very hard-to-see double blaze that signals the sharp left turn.

If you get tired, remember that the inlet just below Crow's Cliff is a perfect place for a final rest. From there the home stretch is easy—about 50 minutes through wooded, well-marked and quite gently undulating terrain. About ten minutes from the parking area you will start to hear the sound of traffic on Highway 69. After such a long and arduous trek, maybe the sounds will be welcome, or maybe you'll feel as I did—rather sad to leave the solitude and tranquility behind.

The Massasauga Provincial Park

Trail Information: The Massasauga Provincial Park has three separate hiking trails—**Wreck Island Trail**, 1.5-kilometres; **Nipissing–North Arm Orienteering Trail**, 30 kilometres; and the **Baker Trail** (see below).

Baker Trail—6.5 kilometre loop, time, 2–3 hours moderate.

Access: From Highway 69, take Muskoka Road 11. Drive north for 6 kilometres, through Mactier, to Healey Lake Road. Pete's Place Access Point is 16.5 kilometres west along Healey Lake Road. Day use access is from the marinas at Woods Bay at the end of the road.

Map: A topographical map of the Massasauga Provincial Park is available from Oastler Lake Provincial Park (705) 378-2401. I strongly urge you to buy it. Trail brochures are also available.

Parking: At the access points.

One of the best kept secrets of the Georgian Bay shores is the Massasauga Provincial Park. Immediately south of Parry Sound and roughly 12 by 21 kilometres in size, it covers 13,050 hectares of rugged shoreline, islands, inland lakes and forest. Its pattern of human history is similar to that of other parks along the Georgian Bay shoreline—a long period of use by aboriginal hunter-gatherers, followed in the nineteenth century by heavy logging, small-scale mining and homesteading. The early- to mid-twentieth century saw the focus change to summer cottage and resort development. However, as the area grew in popularity, an awareness emerged of its unique natural and cultural treasures and also of the urgent need to preserve and look after them. In 1969, the creation of a 607-hectare nature reserve on Moon Island started a land acquisition and conservation process which culminated 20 years later in the establishment of the Massasauga Provincial Park as a Natural Environment Park—a park that is concerned mainly with protecting the natural environment but also with encouraging activities that don't pose a threat to the environment.

Georgian Bay's Eastern Shore

5

So, you won't find any campgrounds for cars or recreational vehicles at Massasauga. The 135 individual campsites scattered throughout the park are pretty basic: each has a tent pad, a privy box, a place for a fire pit and that's it! And what's more, you can only reach the park by water.

Power boats or large sailboats can get into the park from the main boating channel (Port Severn to Parry Sound small-craft route) and may moor overnight in one of the park's seven specially designated anchoring bays. Many parts of the park, however, are not accessible to large craft. If you are a canoeist or a hiker you've got two options. Pete's Place Access Point on the park's southeast boundary leads into Blackstone Harbour. From here you can head north or west to explore some of the quiet inland lakes, or, if you head east, narrow channels will take you through Woods Bay to the main boating channels and out to the windswept, rocky islands along the Georgian Bay shoreline. The Three Legged Lake Access Point, near the park's northeast boundary leads into the undisturbed wilderness of the park's interior lake country. No motorized traffic is allowed, so the only people you'll meet will be travelling either by canoe or on foot!

If you are not a boat owner, don't worry. You can rent a canoe at either of the access points, or, if you prefer to be taken into to the park, take advantage of the water-taxi service (rates vary according to distance and the number of people). The park office at Oastler Lake Provincial Park, (705) 378-2401, takes care of all permits and reservations. If you are a day visitor, you can rent a boat or get taxi service from either Hawksnest Marina, (705) 375-2287, or Moon River Marina, (705) 375-2342, at the end of Woods Bay Road. Again, rates depend on distance; a return trip to Calhoun Lodge cost $30 in 1998.

A splendid topographical map of the park is available from the office. In addition to the cartography, it contains such a wealth of information on the area's history, geology, flora and fauna that I can't imagine trying to use the park without it. The three hiking trails are clearly marked. They vary in length from 1.5 to 30 kilometres, and each affords an opportunity to explore a different aspect of the park's natural or cultural heritage.

For the hiker who loves wilderness camping and rugged terrain, the 30-kilometre **Nipissing–North Arm Orienteering Trail** (there are 10 campsites along the way) offers as much of a challenge as you could possibly want. Starting in the northeast corner of the park at Devil's Elbow, it charts a winding course through undulating terrain, passing through fen and bog, over rock outcrops, ridges and along cliff edges. There is very little cleared trail, and the route, marked by a series of posts, is navigated via compass bearings. (A draft trail guide containing descriptions and compass bearings, is available at the park office.) Obviously, this trail is suitable only for those with experience in orienteering and back-country hiking. However, if you have the requisite skills and stamina, your journey will be filled with interest and diversity as you navigate your way past a stand of 150-year-old white pines, an abandoned copper mine, basking turtles, a great blue heronry, and many other superb bird-watching vantage points. Whatever the time of year, you will not be disappointed.

In terms of length, the **Wreck Island Trail**, on the west boundary of the park, is at the other end of the scale. Although it is just 1.5 kilometres long, it takes the hiker on a fascinating journey through a rugged and utterly spectacular landscape. The park's amazing geological history is nowhere more abundantly evident than on Wreck Island, and this trail takes you to places that have been over a billion years in the making. You'll walk over incredibly twisted and folded rocks that once formed the roots of ancient mountains, and you'll see rocks strung out into dark and light ribbons cut through by bands of pink rock called dykes. You'll pass boulders that have been carried hundreds of kilometres by glacial meltwater and now sit high and dry on top of alien bedrock, and you'll encounter rocks that have been eroded into weird sculptured shapes. An excellent trail guide gives an outline of the area's geo-logical past and explains how the various features came into being. If you are interested in geology, be sure to include this trail in your itinerary.

The park's third trail, the **Baker Trail**, has something for everyone. So, if your time is limited and you can only visit the park for a day, this is the hike to choose. In addition to taking you through some glorious scenery, this walk gives you the opportunity to explore some aspects of the park's human history. Make sure to start rea-sonably early, in any event no later than 11 a.m. Take a picnic and, if it's hot, swimming gear. The terrain is varied, pretty rugged in places, and there is not much flat ground. But there are some spec-tacular views. At 6.5 kilometres, the hike is within the capability of any reasonably fit person.

Baker Trail

The trail starts and ends at Calhoun Lodge, which sits on a rocky promontory on the northeast shore of Blackstone Harbour. The journey by boat from one of the private marinas on Woods Bay takes 15 to 20 minutes and is a delight in itself. The lodge was built in the 1930s and '40s by Joe Calhoun, a lawyer from Ohio, as a summer residence for his family. Today it serves as the park's work headquarters and in the summer season, as a museum. Be sure to pick up an interpretive trail guide either at the park office or the lodge.

At about the time that this book was due to go to print, a decision was taken by the park staff to reblaze the Baker Trail, directing hikers round the loop in a clockwise direction. Reblazing and

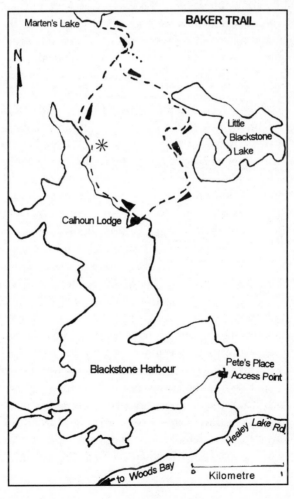

renumbering of the posts is scheduled to be completed by the spring of 2000. No changes have been planned for the trail route. Although I have only walked the loop in a counter-clockwise direction, rewriting the description from a different perspective has not been too difficult. However, as the placement of blazes and posts has not yet been finalized, I have been unable to refer to specific trail markers. The markers will be in place by the spring and the park's own trail guide should also be available by then.

From the lodge, the Baker Trail, which is marked by a series of posts and hiking icons, heads northwest, winding its way through the juniper-clad rocks that top the promontory. After a few minutes it turns toward the water, making a short, sharp descent through trees to lake level. For the next 1.5 kilometres it stays close to the shore, meandering over rocky ground, following the line of the lake slightly above the level of the water. It is a glorious walk with junipers, blueberries, mosses and lichens adorning the rocks underfoot, and long clear views across the water to the rocky, tree-lined shores opposite. Don't forget to stop occasionally and look to the south to take in the seemingly endless vista over Blackstone Harbour.

When you reach the narrows toward the end of the lake, the trail veers right, away from the water. After about 400 metres you'll encounter two crosses at the side of the trail. They mark the burial place of two of the areas early residents, Thomas and Charles Baker. Thomas came with his infant son at the beginning of the nineteenth century, to settle and build up a farm one kilometre north of here (your walk will shortly bring you to the site). For 40 years the family raised cows and grew vegetables. Charles Baker died at the age of 32, when he fell through the ice on Gropp's Marsh, a couple of kilometres southwest of here. Thomas Baker was buried here beside his son 12 years later, in 1944. The two crosses remain as a poignant testament to lives lived and lost in a lonely, unyielding place.

The trail continues in a roughly northern direction and soon brings you alongside an enormous beaver meadow. To the right of the wide, flat path, rocky ground rises abruptly; on the left is the sea of marsh hay which once provided Thomas Baker with a constant supply of animal feed. The meadow seems to go on forever and, in fact, it takes about 25 minutes to travel its length. To the west, on the other side of this "sea" a thickly wooded ridge rises abruptly from the flat plain. When I did the walk in the late fall, it made a glorious backdrop of vividly contrasting greens, yellows and bronzes.

The start of a lonely life?
A log house under construction in the bush, 1880.
Source: Archives of Ontario, Acc 6287 S-8248

The remains of the Baker Farm, at the northern end of the beaver meadow, filled me with unease. The day I was there, there was a thunderstorm, and the site had such a grim and melancholy air that all I could think of was the isolation, the loneliness, the innumerable disappointments and the unending struggle of that family's life. If the sun had been shining, perhaps I would have felt differently. Nature, of course, has not been slow to reassert herself, but, if you search diligently, it is possible to identify old pastures and fields, the remains of a calf shed, an icehouse and the inevitable rock pile.

At the farm site you have several options. Bird watchers will want to take the short trail that continues north for a few metres before curving round sharply to the right. It ends at a large beaver pond that supports an abundance of wildlife, including a heron rookery. If you have more time and are looking for the perfect place for lunch, take the left-hand trail. It leads across low-lying, marshy ground, bringing you, after about 500 metres, to the shores of Marten's Lake. It's a lovely spot; its rocky, tree-lined shores are utterly tranquil, and not even a canoe glides over its waters.

Georgian Bay's Eastern Shore

To continue round the loop, take the right-hand trail. It guides you along a wide, flat path and soon enters a tall deciduous forest. After about 15 minutes the ground starts to become rockier and the path climbs quite steeply. It then descends again into a valley where there is a marsh on your right and water—the end of the north arm of Little Blackstone Lake—on your left.

For the next 1.5 kilometres the trail travels in a largely southerly direction, winding in and out of many dark groves of hemlock, and travelling over very rugged terrain. (When I did this walk from the other direction, I had some trouble following the blazes over this rough stretch; however, the park staff assures me that the new blazing will be much improved.) Be prepared for very little level ground and many short, but very steep ascents and descents. In one or two places, where the path descends very steeply through rocks, you need to be very careful, particularly if the rocks are wet.

A final descent brings you out of the hemlocks and down toward the shore of Little Blackstone Lake. The trail briefly follows the line of the lake before making a right turn onto the wide portage that runs between Little Blackstone Lake and Blackstone Harbour. It's worthwhile going the extra few yards to the left to have a look because Little Blackstone Lake is beautiful, its tree-fringed waters utterly calm and silent.

The home stretch takes you 750 metres through mixed bush. As you near the end, the bush opens up and the waters of Blackstone Harbour come into view. Follow the trail as it makes its final ascent to the top of a rocky promontory, and you're back at Calhoun Lodge.

The Baker Trail is a great way to introduce yourself to the park. From late June to early September Calhoun Lodge is staffed. If you are lucky your visit might coincide with one of the interpretive programs that are offered during the summer. You'll come away knowing more about the Massasauga Provincial Park, and you'll most likely feel that this is a place you want to come back to.

Killbear Provincial Park

Trail Information: **Lighthouse Point Trail**—1.0-kilometre loop, 20 minutes, easy

Twin Points Trail—2-kilometre loop, 45 minutes, easy

Lookout Point Trail—3.5-kilometre loop, 1 hour, easy.

Access: From Highway 69 north of Parry Sound, take District Road 559 west for 19.6 kilometres to Killbear Provincial Park. All park users must pay a fee.

Map: Trail brochures are available from the park office.

Parking: At the trailheads.

Killbear Provincial Park sits on a rocky promontory that guards the narrow entrance to Parry Sound. While no definitive explanation exists for the origin of its name, the Ojibwa name for Killbear Point was Mukwa-Nayosh—"bear kill"—and, indeed, all the myths associated with the naming of Killbear Point seem to have a common theme involving the death of a bear. Bears still live there, but they prefer to keep to the more remote areas, so you are unlikely to see one.

Like the other recreational areas along the Georgian Bay shoreline, the Killbear peninsula has an early and long history of use by First Peoples, and a more recent history of logging and farming. At the turn of the twentieth century, plans to build a resort fortunately never materialized, and the land was bought by the Government of Ontario in 1958.

Today Killbear is one of Ontario's most popular parks, its many visitors drawn to its stunning landscape of verdant forest, windswept pine, juniper-covered rock, and vast expanses of shining water. It's the ideal place for families—883 spacious drive-in campsites; wonderful fishing; mooring and launching facilities for both small and large craft; clear, deep waters that are perfect for divers, snorkellers and swimmers; and more than three kilometres of white sandy beach. For those who want to explore on foot, there are three short and easy hiking trails. You can't possibly get lost, so

Georgian Bay's Eastern Shore

6

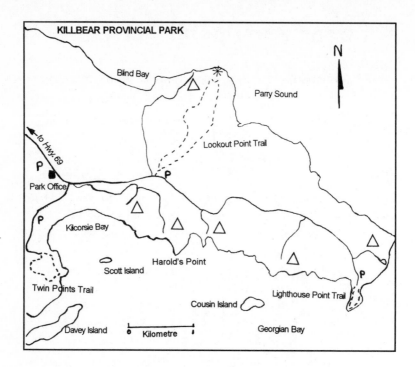

KILLBEAR PROVINCIAL PARK

Blind Bay

Parry Sound

to Hwy. 69

P

Park Office

P

Kilcorsie Bay

Lookout Point Trail

N

Harold's Point

Scott Island

Twin Points Trail

Lighthouse Point Trail

Cousin Island

Davey Island

Kilometre

Georgian Bay

there is no need for me to describe them in detail.

Each trail passes through a different part of the park and each focuses on a different aspect of the park's natural history.

The shortest, **Lighthouse Point Trail**, a 1-kilometre loop, starts at a parking area at the very end of the main park road. The trail follows the shoreline out to the beacon on the rocks at the very tip of the promontory. From the beacon there are wonderful views to the south, across the narrow channel that runs between Killbear Point and Parry Island. The trail continues around the bouldery shoreline, ending at a delightful sandy beach near Lighthouse Campground.

Twin Points Trail takes you on a 2-kilometre loop through mixed forest and over the smooth dome-shaped rocks at the western edge of Kilcorsie Bay. At the start of the hike (at the day use parking area) be sure to pick up the very informative brochure that identifies a number of geological features and explains the various ways in which ice and meltwaters from decaying glaciers have modified the landscape.

Lookout Point Trail starts from a parking area just past the road leading to Blind Bay campground. The route is a 3.5-kilometre loop that takes you through a number of different natural environments to a lookout on the east shore of the Killbear promontory. On the way you'll pass the stumps of some of the great pines that were cut down in this area between 1898 and 1902. This is a lovely walk at any time of the year, but if you happen to be here in the fall, the vista over the blue water to the brilliant hues of the trees on the islands in Parry Sound is unforgettable. Again, be certain to pick up the explanatory booklet at the beginning of the trail—it's well worthwhile.

Although Killbear's easy walks and superb recreational facilities make it the perfect place for families, don't dismiss the park if you are looking for a bit more of a hiking challenge. Killbear is one of the few places in Cottage Country where you can devise a hike to suit your own needs.

Killbear's shoreline, where huge rocks of every size, colour and shape spill down into the water, is a wonderful place to ramble. All you need is a good pair of boots—rock scrambling is hard on the ankles—and a compass. I had one of my most enjoyable Cottage Country hikes in Killbear early in May, before the park was officially open. It was one of those golden weekends when the weather changed overnight from a grey, sullen 10° to a gloriously clear, sunny 25°. We parked at the Lighthouse parking area then set off along the shore in a counter-clockwise direction.

The rock formations along the way are marvellous; the entire journey, in fact, is a vivid and constant demonstration of the tectonic forces that baked, twisted and contorted the earths crust over a billion years ago. Some of the multi-hued rocks are folded horizontally, some vertically; some have alternating bands of pink and dark grey or black; in others the colours run together giving a veined or marbled effect. Where the rocks sink under the water, their colours and patterns seem to come alive, endlessly shifting under the shimmering light of the sun.

We followed the shoreline as far as the campsite at Blind Bay. There we ate lunch on the rocks, looking out over still, clear waters to the groups of islands that dot the Sound. Our journey then continued inland, through woods, following the park roads in a southerly direction. In the heat the leaves of the hardwoods were just starting to uncurl and underneath the trees the ground was carpeted with trilliums. I think we walked about 14 kilometres that day and we didn't meet a soul.

Other Georgian Bay Area Trails

Those interested in wildlife will want to visit Wye Marsh Wildlife Centre on Highway 12 near Midland. The 1,200-hectare marsh supports a diversity of flora and fauna and is accessible by boardwalk and canoe. There are trails, guided walks and many interpretive programs. For information call (705) 526-7809.

The Five Winds Ski Touring Club maintains a series of marked wilderness trails north of McCrae Lake, accessible from Muskoka Road 32. Like McCrae Lake, these will be very rugged trails, suitable only for very experienced and fit hikers. To have any success in finding and negotiating these trails, you must buy the map of the Gibson Trail System, available from the Five Winds Ski Touring Club at (416) 635-2702.

The Massasauga Provincial Park and Georgian Bay Islands National Park offer secluded boat-in campsites. Awenda and Killbear Provincial Parks have superb drive-in sites for family camping. Oastler Lake Provincial Park, on Highway 69, 8 kilometres south of Parry Sound also has drive-in campsites.

There is a wide variety of places to stay in the Midland–Penetanguishene area and the Parry Sound area—motels, lodges and B&Bs. See page 149 for useful contact numbers.

I can heartily recommend No.1 Jury Drive Bed and Breakfast in Penetanguishene. It's right at the entrance of Discovery Harbour and is open from May to October. Crista van Bruggen will give you a warm welcome and a good breakfast, and may even lend you a bicycle so that you can explore the many historical sights that Penetang has to offer.

Central Cottage Country

Hiking in the central part of Cottage Country is not quite as straightforward as hiking in the other three regions. If you look for Provincial Parks on a map of Ontario, you'll notice that on the southern part of the Shield, between Highway 11 and Highway 41, (excluding Algonquin Park) they are rather sparse and widely scattered, apart from a fairly tight cluster immediately to the southeast of Algonquin. Within this particular cluster, most parks stretch out along the shoreline of a river. These places are great if you are an intrepid, white-water canoeist, but not so great if you want to hike.

There is a reason for the relative scarcity of sizable provincial parks—the land immediately north of the Kawartha Lakes and around the Muskoka Lakes is the most densely populated and highly developed land on the southern Shield. Travel and transportation, made easy by the large navigable lakes, meant that the area was settled early and that tourism was well developed by the end of the nineteenth century. By the early 1950s, when the government was looking for suitable parkland, an exhaustive search of these areas revealed that little suitable land remained.

In other areas, however, it was a different story. In the places distant from large, navigable lakes, poor roads delayed settlement. Even after the advent of the railway had made travel easier, settlement remained slow and scattered—always closely tied to the waxing and waning of the lumber and mining industries. So, when parkland was needed, it's not surprising that suitable lands were found in these less-developed areas.

Happily, the provincial parks in Central Cottage Country afford splendidly varied hiking opportunities: Arrowhead's four trails vary in length from 1 to 7 kilometres; at Petroglyphs, there are four hikes, ranging from 3 to 13 kilometres; Silent Lake's trails range from 1.5 to 15 kilometres; Bon Echo's from 2 to 17 kilometres. In each park you can discover something unusual or dramatic, be it a panoramic view from the top of a 120-metre cliff, ancient rock carvings and paintings, or an osprey's nest high in the branches of a dead tree in the middle of a pond.

Provincial parks are not the only places to hike. If you take another look at your map, on the border of Muskoka and Haliburton Counties, a few kilometres south of Dorset, you may see an arrow labelled Leslie. M. Frost Natural Resources Centre pointing to the head of St. Nora Lake. It's such a discreet label; there is nothing to indicate that it is pointing the way to 24,000 hectares of magnificent forest and lake country. With only 7 percent of its total area under private ownership, the Frost Centre is a paradise for outdoor enthusiasts.

There are other options, too. In recent years, there has been a growing awareness of the lack of obvious places to hike in central Muskoka. So, the Muskoka Recreational Trails Council has produced a list of additional places to hike in Muskoka. Some of the trails are multi-use, some rather urban, but some are well worthwhile exploring, and the fact that the brochure exists at all demonstrates a real desire on the part of local organizations to make more of Muskoka available to the walker.

Resorts, too, should not be discounted. The heyday of the grand hotels may be over, but resorts still thrive throughout the area. I have listed a few that have their own hiking trails.

And finally, there is the legacy of the railway era. Several of the lines that bludgeoned their way optimistically through rock, hill and swamp at the end of the nineteenth century, only to fall silent once the lumber or iron ore was gone, have taken on a new life as recreational trails. In Cottage Country's central area, the 156-kilometre Hastings Heritage Trail runs from Glen Ross all the way to Lake St. Peter. Along its route you can explore the ghosts of long-disappeared mining towns and communities that grew up overnight, following a rumour of gold. When you reach Bancroft, take the opportunity to do a bit of mining yourself. Although all of Bancroft's mines have closed, the enthusiasm for rockhounding remains, and the staff at the Mineral Museum lead mineral-gathering tours several times a week. If you continue toward the end of the old railway line, you'll be rewarded by some very wild and rugged scenery.

So, to hike successfully in Cottage Country's central area, you may have to plan a little more carefully but, without a doubt, there is some very good hiking to be found.

Arrowhead Provincial Park

Trail Information: There are 16 kilometres of hiking trails in the park.

Mayflower Lake–Homesteader's Trail— 4.5-kilometre loop, 2 hours, moderate

Beaver Meadow Trail— 7-kilometre loop, 3 hours, moderate

Access: On Highway 11, drive 8 kilometres north of Huntsville. Exit on the east side, at the park entrance. All park users must pay a fee.

Map: Free information and trail guides are available at the Park Office.

Parking: Near the start of each trail.

Arrowhead Provincial Park is a wonderful place for a family vacation. Within its 1,237 hectares, there are high wooded hills, two sparkling lakes, two rivers, long sandy beaches and a waterfall. Both day visitors and campers get a warm welcome. But remember that this is one of Ontario's busiest parks. If you want to camp you must book ahead. Its 338 spacious and private drive-in campsites make camping very pleasant and easy. And once you've settled in, there is no shortage of things to do. Arrowhead Lake has wonderful swimming beaches and picnic areas, and its park naturalists run a series of diverse programs. Canoeists can explore long stretches of quiet water, fishermen can pit their wits against wily speckled trout and bass on both lakes (no motorboats allowed), and those who like to explore on foot can choose from among its four hiking trails.

The trails, being neither long nor difficult, make Arrowhead Park an ideal place for the inexperienced hiker to make a start. Each trail, moreover, has its own distinct character. Two are very short: the 1-kilometre Mayflower Lake Trail explores the shoreline of the smaller of the two lakes, and the 2-kilometre Stubbs Falls Trail takes you through forest to the spot where the Little East River plunges down a 9-metre rock chute. The 3-kilometre Homesteader's Trail passes along the route of an early settlement road and visits the remains of an old homestead. The longest trail, the Beaver Meadow Trail, winds along the wooded ridges at the

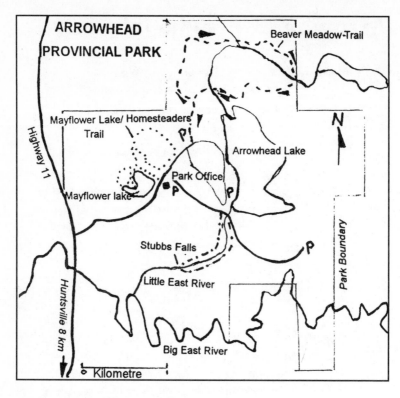

northern end of the park, through the wetlands of the Little East River Valley and past another homestead site.

Mayflower Lake–Homesteader's Trail

The Mayflower Lake Trail and Homesteader's Trail can be combined to make a very pleasant 4-kilometre loop, full of interest and variety. Park at the rear of the information booth and walk back to Mayflower Lake, where you will see a trail sign. A steep bank leads down to the shore where you turn right to follow the trail around the edge. It's an exceptionally pretty lake—water lilies adorn the shallows, and frogs croak an accompaniment as you pass.

At the end of the lake, the trail moves inland a little to avoid wet ground but, as the whole area is very marshy, you are well advised to wear waterproof boots. Look for the beaver lodge just offshore. Once round the end of the lake, the trail starts to climb a little, taking you through lovely mixed woods: maple, birch and some very old pine. The path follows the line of the lake at a slight elevation and after a few minutes descends toward water level. When the trail moves out of the deep shade of the tall trees, you'll notice an increase in the amount of undergrowth; by midsummer, the ferns are shoulder height.

The path makes a sharp right turn as it nears the dam on the west shore. Here, the surface of the lake is like glass, and many downed trees lie submerged among water lilies and cattails. You make quite a steep ascent at the end of the lake as the trail curves round to the right then heads back in a northerly direction. About 30 minutes from the start you reach the amphitheatre.

If this brief trek has whetted your appetite, you can start out from here on the Homesteader's Trail. Cross in front of the amphitheatre to a hiking icon fixed to a tree in the northwest corner. This path heads northwest through mixed woods, over a gently undulating landscape that in June is carpeted with bunchberry and Canada mayflower. You soon pass through a small, partially cleared area where daisies, hawkweeds and wild strawberries thrive in the patches of sunshine. Then it's back into deep shade.

After about 20 minutes, you reach a sign pointing right to the Iris Bog Loop. My advice is not to miss it, provided that you have good boots—the word "bog" is not a misnomer. This side trail lengthens the hike a bit, but it's so magical and mysterious that it's worth every extra step. (If you choose not to explore the Iris Bog Loop, continuing along the trail will take you around the Homesteader's Trail in the opposite direction.)

Along the Iris Bog Loop the path soon brings you into a wet, cool, green world where ferns and sedges rise from the edge of little pools among moss-covered, jumbled outcrops of rock. If you happen to be there in June, you will be surrounded by patches of deep blue—the flag irises in bloom.

The vegetation is very dense but, if you keep a sharp eye open for the hiking icon on trees as you pass through the bog, you can't go far wrong, and, after 15 minutes or so, you'll find yourself on drier ground. Just after the trail passes through a stand of large scotch pine, you reach the amphitheatre parking lot.

Take the amphitheatre access road down to the main park road and turn left. Just past the Lumby Campgrounds intersection, take the trail that veers left into the tall woods. A boardwalk takes you over wet ground, and then you start a gradual ascent past several rocky outcrops. The path is not difficult to hike over, but when you remember that this was once the only road, you'll tend to see it in a different light. In fact, there was no road at all until the 1870s.

Central Cottage Country

Not a smooth ride, but better than nothing.
A early road through Shield country.
Source: Archives of Ontario, S 17349

At the highest point, you get a glimpse of Arrowhead Lake on the right. The descent brings you to more boardwalk, after which the trail veers left into an area that has obviously once been cleared. This is all that remains of the homestead founded in the 1870s by Mr. William Lunt. Not much remains now: a stone wall, a pile of rocks, and if you look carefully, an apple tree and raspberry bushes—mute and barely discernible remains of an attempt to wrest a living from harsh and unyielding land.

You reach the Iris Bog intersection about five minutes after the homestead. Then it takes about 15 more to retrace your steps back to the amphitheatre and the end of your hike.

Beaver Meadow Trail

The Beaver Meadow Trail is Arrowhead's longest hike. While it is neither long nor difficult, it does take you through a very active beaver habitat, so it is one of the trails that may change from year to year, depending on what the beavers have been up to. In any event, a good pair of waterproof boots are essential for this walk. It is nonetheless, a lovely trail—one which offers a great variety of terrains and wildlife.

You'll find the trailhead on the park road that skirts round the north side of Lumby Campground. Park on the shoulder. The trail follows a wide cart track north through mixed bush. Keep left when the trail forks after 300 hundred metres or so. Wildflowers grow in profusion by the side of the path: in early summer, ranunculus, daisy, hawkweed and Jacob's ladder vie for your attention; in the fall, golden rod and asters line your route.

After passing through a very attractive, half-cleared area ringed with dark conifers, you enter more mature woods. In summer, ferns carpet the ground and the tall trees cast ever-changing patterns of dappled light and shade. After following a very pleasant, gently undulating route through the trees for a further kilometre or so, you reach a sign pointing the way to a lookout. A short path takes you to a large rock where you can look out through trees toward the wooded ridge that forms the north side of the Little East River valley.

After the lookout, the trail starts to descend and soon brings you out of the forest. You now enter the vast flat, marshy area where several branches of the Little East River converge before entering Arrowhead Lake. For the next two and a half kilometres the trail is likely to be very wet. It could also be completely flooded and strewn with downed trees and other debris, for this is beaver territory and beavers respect neither boardwalk nor trail signs. When I took this trail, a large portion of boardwalk near the beginning of the meadow had been completely flooded over by a brand new dam built in the early spring. However, the park staff is pretty quick to post flood-warning notices when the beavers' building program becomes a bit too enthusiastic.

The trail winds eastward around the perimeter of the beaver meadow. Most of the time, you walk over uneven ground, with wooded terrain rising on your left and the flat, marshy meadow on your right. About half way around, the trail divides and offers you a choice: continue on the main trail, or take a short side trail that heads off to the right to a lookout over the beaver meadow and rejoins the main path a little further on. Soon after this detour, the trail crosses a bridge over a creek and, after winding through more marshy ground, emerges suddenly into a very large, sunny meadow ringed with dark trees.

There don't appear to be any trail signs here and, as several paths crisscross the meadow, you may feel a bit confused. However, you won't go far wrong if you stick to a faint trail on the right-hand side which follows the treeline. As you make your way across the open land, it's not difficult to imagine animals grazing, and homesteaders painstakingly tending to their crops, planting a garden and hoping against hope that they will produce enough to survive on. I saw no signs of the homestead, but the path does bring you very close to an ancient lilac tree that perhaps stood near the house.

Beyond the lilac, you'll see a blue hiking icon on a wide trail that runs east-west across the southern end of the meadow. Turn right at the icon. After a few minutes, you will catch a glimpse of Arrowhead Lake through the trees on your left. The trail continues to head west over the flat terrain at the lake's end and, after about 20 minutes, it brings you to the intersection with the trail coming in from the road. Turn left and retrace your steps to your car.

If you have started your walk fairly early in the day, you'll have plenty of time to go to the lake for a picnic and a swim. And, if you *still* have time, you can take a very pleasant walk to Stubbs Falls. From the parking area at the southwest end of Arrowhead Lake, an easy trail heads west for a kilometre, following the course of the Little East River through the forest. The ground underfoot becomes rockier, and you start to notice very large white pines among the hardwoods. With very little warning, the river, which has been quietly ambling along, makes a headlong plunge down a 9-metre rocky chute into a deep ravine. A bridge takes you across the river and sets you on the way back to the start along the other bank. The Stubbs Falls hike can be completed in about 40 minutes.

Leslie M. Frost Natural Resources Centre

Trail Information: There are 8.3 kilometres of hiking trails on the east side of Highway 35, and 22 kilometres of cross country ski trails on the west side.
Lakeshore–Acclimatization–Steep Rock Loop—6-kilometre loop, 2.5 hours, moderate

Access: From Highway 35 at Minden, drive north for 35 kilometres. From Highway 35 at Dorset, drive south for 12 kilometres. The Frost Centre campus is on the east side of Highway 35, on St. Nora Lake.

Map: Free information and trail guides are available at the office. You may also buy a topographical map of the Frost Centre Area.

Parking: At the Frost Centre

Toward the end of the nineteenth century, travel through the isolated, rocky terrain along the upper part of the Bobcaygeon Road was fraught with difficulty, and consequently, settlement was slow. The lumber companies, of course, had a keen interest in exploiting the richly forested land in the headwaters of the Black and Gull Rivers. For many years extensive logging took place—first the stands of white pine, later maple, yellow birch and hemlock.

When the timber boom was over, 24,000 hectares of land remained under Crown ownership. In the 1950s and 1960s, it served as the training ground for forest rangers enrolled in the University of Toronto's forestry school at the head of St. Nora Lake and, in 1974, after the forestry program had been taken over by community colleges, the Ontario Ministry of Natural Resources opened this site as a residential outdoor education centre—the Leslie M. Frost Natural Resources Centre.

With one third of its area covered by water, the Frost Centre is a paradise for canoeists. However, those who prefer to travel on foot will find a network of trails and numerous unofficial roads and tracks. On the east side of Highway 35, near the Frost Centre headquarters, there are a number of fairly short but quite varied hiking loops,

8

ranging from easy to rugged. On the west side of the highway, its 22 kilometres of cross country ski trails make ideal hiking trails in the spring, summer and fall.

The Frost Centre produces a number of very useful brochures. At the administration building you can pick up free leaflets about their day hiking trails, ski trails, forest management strategies, local geology and wildlife viewing. Staff members are helpful, very knowledgeable and pleased to advise on the state of the trails and assist in planning an appropriate route.

Lakeshore–Acclimatization–Steep Rock Loop

In the parking lot at the south end of the Frost Centre campus you'll find a large display map. The walk described here incorporates parts of three trails marked there: Lakeshore (marked with yellow trail signs), Acclimatization (red) and Steep Rock (green). (It also takes you past posts 2 to 10 of the Geomorphology Hike. If you are at all interested in geology make sure to pick up the brochure for this hike.)

From the car park, head north through the campus along a path close to the lake. After about ten minutes you'll cross Ranger Creek and reach the start of the trail system. The trail follows the shoreline on a slightly elevated path through mixed woods. After about 100 metres, you reach the intersection where the yellow Lakeshore Trail branches right to circle around the headland jutting out into St. Nora Lake. It's a worthwhile detour and takes only about fifteen minutes. The trail travels along the shore and gives wonderful views over the water.

After the detour the trail leaves the lake and enters deciduous forest. Two or three minutes later, it rejoins the Acclimatization Trail. The Geomorphology Hike's Post 2, close by, marks the final resting place of a large rock, called a glacial float, that was gouged from its original bedrock by an advancing glacier and carried along before being deposited by meltwater when the glacier decayed.

About 300 metres further along the trail, bear right toward the lake, following the green signs of the Steep Rock Trail. After only a few minutes you begin to pass along the bottom of a high, very steep rock outcrop. The chaotic jumble of rock fragments lying at its base is a forceful reminder that erosion is a never-ending process. If you happen to be on the trail in winter, you tend to tread a little warily, hoping that the frost will not send any chunks of rock face hurtling downwards just as you pass.

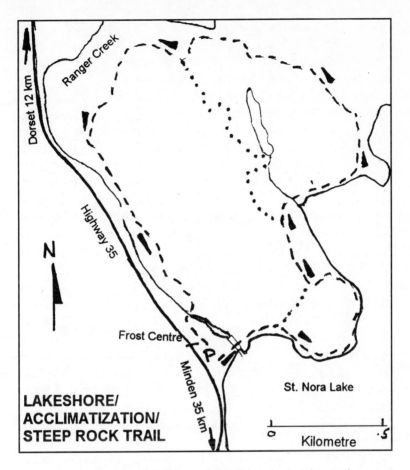

Map labels:
Dorset 12 km
Ranger Creek
Highway 35
N
Frost Centre
P
Minden 35 km
St. Nora Lake
LAKESHORE/
ACCLIMATIZATION/
STEEP ROCK TRAIL
0
Kilometre
.5

As it approaches the shore of the lake again, the trail passes along a wide rock ledge. The brochure describes how this particular piece of rock face was formed and how it came to have a layered, wave-like appearance. A few minutes later, you arrive at Post 5 of the Geomorphology Hike.

The trail continues along the rocky ledge for another 100 metres or so. Just before turning away from the lake edge it passes underneath a great shelf of rock—almost like a cave—with ferns and mosses clinging to its surface. On your right, a tiny, rocky, promontory juts out into the lake. In summer this is the perfect lunch spot—right in the path of any cooling breeze.

Once again the trail takes you north, bringing you shortly to more open, airy woods where the large mature trees cast an ever-shifting filigree of light and shade. After a few minutes, when the trail divides, take the left branch (Dawson Ponds Trail continues north). The path makes a gentle ascent, crossing the course of a stream twice, and then it veers left after the second crossing. After climbing for about 250 metres, it begins to descend, steeply at first, then more gently. Very soon it veers north, and after about 100 metres, brings you to the foot of a huge, sheer cliff.

When you turn your back to the cliff you realize that you are standing on the edge of a very large swamp. To a non-geologist, the juxtaposition of these two completely different landforms may seems surprising, but if you consult the Geomorphology Hike brochure you will find that they are complementary. Briefly, the swamp sits over a fault—a fracture between two portions of the earth's crust. When movement occurs along a fault, it leaves an area of loose, unstable rock that is more easily shifted than the stable rock around it. So, when the glaciers pushed their way down from the north they gouged out the soft, looser rock, cutting a deep channel which is now filled by the swamp.

The trail skirts around the north end of the swamp and after about 300 metres, presents you with a choice. If you turn left, the Steep Rock Trail will take you south for about one kilometre, along the lower, western border of the swamp valley, to rejoin the Acclimatization Trail near the lake. If you choose this route you'll get some good views of the steep cliffs on the east side of the valley. The right fork (the Acclimatization Trail) curves round to the west, then south to pass along the edge of much flatter terrain beside Ranger Creek. Either way the distance is just short of two kilometres.

On a winter or early spring hike, I prefer to take the right fork. The ground levels off quite soon after the intersection, and the trail takes you through very beautiful, mature forest for about 500 metres before descending to the river valley.

The walk back alongside the river is very pretty, particularly during the spring thaw, just before the snow and ice have completely melted—a rocky, tree-clad hillside rising on your left, and to your right, the river, sedate and demure during most of the year, but now swollen with melting snow, enjoying a brief, glorious fling as it dashes headlong toward the lake. After 200 metres, a bridge takes you over the river, and a short stroll through the Frost Centre campus brings you back to your car.

Petroglyphs Provincial Park

Trail Information: Trails in the park and surrounding area cover 18 kilometres.

High Falls Trail—6.5-kilometre linear trail (13 kilometres in all) 4–5 hours, moderate to strenuous

Access: From Highway 28, north of Burleigh Falls, turn east along Northey's Bay Road. After 11 kilometres, you will see the park entrance on the north side of the road. All park users must pay a fee.

Map: Free information and trail guides are available at the Park Office.

Parking: At the start of the trail leading to the petroglyph site.

Petroglyphs Provincial Park covers 1,550 hectares of land, just to the north of Stoney Lake. This area has the characteristic rugged Shield landscape of forest, wetland, small lakes and rocky ridges. But although it may look like many other parks on the southern Shield, this park has something that sets it apart from the rest—it is home to one of the most important archaeological sites in Canada. Among the tall hardwood trees, on a large, flattish dome of white marble, are hundreds of petroglyphs—rock carvings—made between 500 and 1,000 years ago by Algonkian-speaking peoples.

The symbolic carvings, which are believed to have deep spiritual meaning, take many forms: animals, such as birds, turtles and snakes; strangely curved boats, quite unlike the birch-bark canoes that the natives would have used; shaman figures; a spirit called Nanabush, who could take any form, depicted here as a rabbit; and a large figure thought to represent Gitcha Manitou or the Great Spirit. To members of the Ojibwa Nation, who are the guardians of the carvings, this is a sacred site. Believing that the figures have wisdom to impart to all who visit, they call the site, "the rocks that teach."

Obviously, your first walk in the park will be to the petroglyphs. A clearly marked 1-kilometre trail leads from the parking area, taking you first over juniper-clad rocks then through trees. Today, the rock is by necessity protected from the elements, happily by an

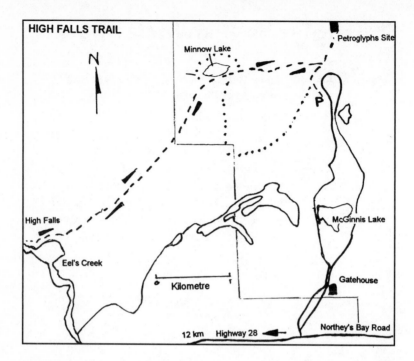

N

Minnow Lake

Petroglyphs Site

P

High Falls

Eel's Creek

McGinnis Lake

Kilometre

Gatehouse

12 km   Highway 28

Northey's Bay Road

architecturally stunning building. Its tall glass walls and roof keep the sense of confinement to a minimum; light pours in unimpeded and, on a clear day, the sun's rays, filtered through the tall forest canopy, cast shimmering patterns on the face of the rock.

Inside the building, First Nations guides are on hand to interpret the carvings and answer questions. If you are timely, you might witness a tobacco ceremony, performed by Ojibwa elders. In any event, you will notice their gifts of tobacco placed here and there amongst the figures. Responses to the carvings are very individual, but each time I have visited, I have been fascinated by the place and strangely moved by the experience.

Once you have seen the petroglyphs, retrace your steps to a large map of the park trails. Each of several trails, ranging in length from 3 to 13 kilometres, is named and marked with its own colour. All of the trails are delightful, but if you are up for a fairly long, challenging walk, the High Falls Trail is the one to choose. It heads west past Minnow Lake, through forest and wetland, beyond the boundary of the park, into the Peterborough Crown Game Reserve, to bring you to a spectacular high, rocky plateau where Eel's Creek plunges through a rocky cleft to a pool below. It is not a loop trail. You must retrace your steps back into the park, but this is no hardship; on the homeward journey, the landscape, seen from a new perspective, looks quite different.

High Falls Trail

This trail is marked by a blue disk and, for the first part of the hike, shares its path with the Nanabush Trail and Marsh Trail.

The well-blazed trail makes a gentle descent over rocky, undulating terrain, through immature conifers. After about ten minutes, you will cross over a cattail marsh on a boardwalk. A viewing station gives you good vistas of the marsh, its surrounding meadow and the dramatic, dark ring of trees at its edge. If you are there in late summer, clusters of purple asters and goldenrod add splashes of colour to the scene.

Beyond the boardwalk, the trail passes through some beautiful stands of silver birch. When it divides (about 25 minutes into the hike), stay left. After a few minutes of walking through tall, mature, mixed woods, you reach a boardwalk that skirts around the edge of a lily pond. A hundred metres or so further on, the Marsh Trail goes off to the left. Keep right, and just beyond the intersection you'll encounter a snake icon at the edge of the trail. From here, a short trail leads to the edge of Minnow Lake. It's an exceptionally beautiful lake, so the brief detour is worth making.

The path leads up to a slightly elevated point that looks north over the tree-ringed lake. The rock beneath you is covered with a blanket of pine needles shed by an enormously tall pine that stands like a sentinel at the very edge. On the north shore, where huge rocks spill into the water, cedar, spruce and juniper maintain a precarious existence, clinging to an inhospitable host. Water lilies cover the lake's calmest spots and embellish the deep blue surface with patches of white and yellow embroidery. It's a perfect rest spot!

Back on the High Falls Trail, you journey alongside the lake, getting intermittent glimpses of water and rocky shelves. Shortly after the trail begins a descent, the Nanabush Trail branches off to the right. Stay left, and after a few minutes you'll come to steep rocky ledge. It is not difficult to clamber down, but you need to take care, particularly if it's wet. (This is one of the reasons why I strongly recommend boots for this hike.) By now, the landscape has become more open, and the trail winds through lichen and moss-covered rocks, tall ferns and, in late summer, asters and goldenrod. Along this stretch, you leave the provincial park and enter the Peterborough Crown Game Preserve.

After you have been walking for about an hour (nearing the halfway point) the trail passes through a very wet area. At some time in the past, logs were laid to keep the hiker above the worst of the

Central Cottage Country

95

muck. Alas, those logs are now virtually submerged and you need to find a stout stick to help you keep your balance as you teeter across what is essentially a greasy pole in the middle of a quagmire!

After the tricky crossing, you travel through pleasant, open countryside and, about half an hour later, you arrive at a bridge over a small stream. Once over the bridge, the path ascends sharply. The terrain is still rocky and the path heavily strewn with tree roots, but you are now passing through more open, airy, mature, mixed forest. About twenty-five minutes after the bridge, you'll glimpse water through the trees to your left. As the trail approaches a very pretty lake (a broadening of Eel's Creek) you'll notice a high cliff on your right. The trail charts a course between the lake and the cliff before turning toward the cliff. Then, a brief and not-too-arduous scramble brings you out onto a vast rocky plateau at the top of the falls.

It's a dramatic setting. Tall pines, cedars, and a variety of mature deciduous trees rise from clefts in the huge, whale-backed rocks. Here, Eel's Creek, after meandering gently through the countryside at plateau-level, plunges through a narrow cleft in the Precambrian rock, falling in a series of spectacular chutes into a pool. There are numerous places to sit in the shade, eat a picnic and watch either the falls or the many canoeists who find this a challenging place to test their skills. But watch out for poison ivy.

When you are ready to leave, retrace your route back to the park. Each time I make the homeward trek, I find myself thinking about the early aboriginal peoples. Did they leave their birch-bark canoes at the top of High Falls? Did they head east along this very trail to their most sacred site?

When you approach Minnow Lake, if you have the energy, there are a couple of opportunities to explore new ground. The first is to follow the north shore of Minnow Lake by taking the Nanabush Trail, which heads left, crossing a boardwalk over wetland, at the west end of the lake. It then ascends quite sharply to reach the top of the north shore. The path runs through trees, following the edge of the lake, and about halfway along brings you to a fine lookout on a grassy knoll high above the water, with wonderful views of the south shore. It's an ideal place for a brief rest before you set out on the final stretch.

Another option is to remain on the High Falls Trail for about 300 metres beyond the Nanabush Trail intersection, and then to take the Marsh Trail. It first heads south, then sweeps around a large wetland area before heading north to rejoin the High Falls Trail, just before the parking area. It will add about 2 kilometres to the hike.

High atop one of many clifftop lookouts in Algonquin Provincial Park.
—Kevin Callan

*Silver-white streams and rust-toned leaves
mark autumn in the Kawarthas.*

—Kevin Callan

Autumn reflections on Slide Lake, Frontenac Provincial Park.
—John Legget

*Overlooking Fairy Lake from Beausoleil Island,
Georgian Bay Islands National Park.*
—Willy Waterton

Algonquin Park, a favourite family destination.
—Kevin Callan

A hiker pauses to enjoy a view of Big Salmon Lake,
Frontenac Provincial Park.

—R. Turrall

Muskoka—beyond the famous cottages.
—Kevin Callan

*Setting off across the rugged western end of Wreck Island,
Massasauga Provincial Park.*

Silent Lake Provincial Park

Trail Information: The park's 3 hiking trails cover 19.5 kilometres.

Lakeshore Trail—15-kilometre loop
6–7 hours, strenuous

Access: From Highway 28, 80 kilometres north of Peterborough, or 24 kilometres south of Bancroft. The entrance to Silent Lake Provincial Park is on the east side of the Highway. All park users must pay a fee.

Map: Free information and trail guides are available at the Gatehouse.

Parking: At the day use parking area.

Work on the first colonization road to run through the empty Shield country north of Burleigh Falls started in 1860. Hopes must have been high after J.W. Ferguson, the surveyor, proffered the optimistic prediction that the land alongside the proposed Burleigh Road would become "in the course of a few years, the most prosperous of any of the new Colonization Roads...and [would] yield to the industrious husbandman a profitable return for his labour."

As it turned out, his optimism was misplaced. As early as 1866, there were bitter complaints about the road's "irregular, tortuous and injudicious location"; settlement along the adjoining land was slow, and the road never developed the importance of some of the other colonization roads.

One group of settlers who almost certainly would have travelled along this difficult thoroughfare was the Patterson family who came in the latter part of the nineteenth century to farm land in the extreme southeast corner of Haliburton County, at the head of Silent Lake. The logging companies, of course, would have been there before them, arriving in the middle of the century, to cut first the great white pine, then the remaining hardwoods and softwoods. Perhaps the opportunity to make some extra income from logging helped the Pattersons to survive, at least for a time. But, by the 1920s, all the usable trees had been felled, and the saws were silent; the loggers had moved on, and the homestead stood empty.

Central Cottage Country

10

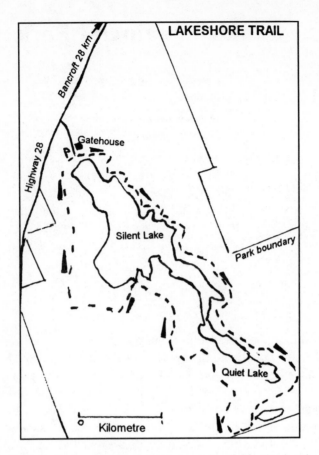

LAKESHORE TRAIL

Bancroft 28 km

Highway 28

Gatehouse

Silent Lake

Park boundary

Quiet Lake

Kilometre

In their wake, a wealthy American arrived, liked what he saw and built a lodge. For the next 40 years, Silent Lake, now a favourite haunt of sportsmen, echoed with the sound of hunting rifles. Happily, in 1967, the lodge and 1,420 hectares of surrounding land were acquired by the government. Finally, for the first time in more than a hundred years, Silent Lake was truly silent.

Today, Highway 28, which mainly follows the course of the old Burleigh Road, is very busy. However, the moment you pull off the road into Silent Lake Provincial Park, you find that you have entered a serene and beautiful place where a lot of care has been taken to conserve the wild and rugged landscape.

The park is undeveloped and remains, as far as is possible, in a natural state; priority is given to activities that are compatible with conserving the natural environment. One hundred and sixty-seven campsites—nearly all accessible to motor vehicles—are completely hidden among the trees on the north side of the lake. From the day use area at the head of the lake, the rocky shoreline and rugged,

Skidding logs across a frozen lake to await the spring thaw.
Source: Archives of Ontario, C120 -3 S-5180

forested hills look as if they have never been disturbed. Here and there, a canoe glides over the surface of the lake (motor boats are not allowed). Visitors may rent a canoe, fish for trout or smallmouth and largemouth bass, swim from one of three sandy beaches, cycle along a mountain-bike trail, or hike along one of the three trails.

These trails range in length from 1.5 to 15 kilometres. The shortest and easiest, ideal for beginners or families with young children, is the 1.5-kilometre Lakehead Loop Trail. It starts near the gatehouse, at the bridge over Silent Creek, follows the shoreline of the lake to a vantage point overlooking the lake, and then circles back to the start, through stands of hemlock, sugar maple and red oak.

The 3-kilometre Bonnie's Pond Trail is a moderately rugged trail that explores wetland and forest on the east side of the lake. Its name harks back to the park's early logging days and the unfortunate death of one of the horses that moved the great pine logs by skidding them across frozen water. Here, a horse named Bonnie drowned when the spring ice gave way, and since then, the pond has been known as Bonnie's Pond. Starting at the Pincer Bay parking area, the trail makes a wide curve north then east, toward a large beaver pond, once the site of log skidding. From the pond, the path heads over rock and through forest to a spectacular lookout point above the lake before returning to the starting point.

The third trail, the Lakeshore Trail, is for the fit and experienced hiker only. It makes a 15-kilometre circuit around the lake, passing through beaver meadows, swamps, hardwood forest and, at times, over very rugged terrain. Wonderful views make it a memorable experience. In hot weather, this trail will take you an entire day, so be sure to start early and take plenty of water. There is an option: after about 6 kilometres, you can head back along a less rugged cross country ski trail. However, even if you take this shortcut, you will still cover about 12 kilometres overall, and a fair level of fitness is still required.

Lakeshore Trail

The trail begins at the day use area. Follow the blue markers across the bridge over Silent Creek. A wide path heads through tall, mature trees to the edge of the lake, then follows the shoreline. (The Lakehead Loop shares this first part of the walk.) A line of trees stands between you and the water, but there are excellent views of the lake. After a few minutes, you pass through a grove of very tall hemlocks. A little further on, when the trail divides, keep right, along the shore. After 200 metres, a boardwalk takes you over a marshy area.

A half an hour's walk will bring you to a bench overlooking the lake from a rocky outcrop. You are now passing through an attractive beach area near the Pincer Bay Campground. Just past the beach, a short rocky ascent takes you to a vantage point overlooking the lake. This area is crisscrossed with small trails leading from the campsites, and it's not totally clear which is the official hiking trail, but if you hug the shoreline, you can't go far wrong.

After 15 minutes, Bonnie's Pond Trail goes off to the left. Shortly afterwards, you descend into a magical gorge strewn with jumbled rocks, mosses and wonderful ferns. After ascending the other side, the trail continues its rocky course along the shoreline, passing through tall pine and hemlock.

When you've been walking for just over an hour and are perhaps feeling like a bit of a break, you emerge onto a tiny, rocky promontory where a couple of rustic seats command a glorious view of the lake. There's a small rocky island just offshore, and a narrow arm of the lake on your left. Don't stay too long though, because you've only covered about 3.5 kilometres, a quarter of the distance.

Back on the trail, after about five minutes, the path leaves the shoreline, veering left to climb, quite steeply, through balsam and hemlock, to higher ground. Here hardwoods mingle with the conifers. Quite soon, the trail descends again to the shoreline and emerges at the water's edge, opposite the most perfect rocky island, crowned with pines and cranberry bushes. After a further ten minutes, the trail descends into wetland, taking you past pickerel weed and cattail, and a splendid beaver dam. (The lake, by this time, has become very narrow.)

Just before you reach the end of the main body of the lake, the trail emerges onto a rocky, elevated lookout, crowned with pines and cedars and carpeted with soft pine needles. The water is deep and there is easy entry so, on a hot day, it's a perfect place (and your last chance) for a cooling dip. But, again, don't stop for too long because, even though you've been walking for about two and a quarter hours, you've only covered about six kilometres.

Shortly after the trail leaves the lookout, it moves away from the shore and briefly joins a wider, cross country ski trail, which comes in from the left. Anyone who is beginning to feel tired should take this opportunity to drop out here and head back left—it's a 6-kilometre hike back to the Gatehouse.

If you continue on the main trail, you soon begin to cross the low wetlands between Silent Lake and its neighbour, Quiet Lake. A boardwalk takes you over a particularly wet area, then the trail veers to the left, climbing up the side of a rocky creek, past a beaver dam. You are now approaching Quiet Lake, which is almost completely covered with vegetation. Thick carpets of water lilies give way to cedar swamp as you progress around the lake, and in places the path tends to be very wet.

At the end of the lake, the trail follows the course of the connecting stream. When the trail cuts through a rocky gorge, it continues to run parallel to the stream, at a slightly elevated position. Within a couple of minutes you'll catch sight of the next little lake.

Now that you are past the halfway point, it's time for a well-earned rest, so look for a very large rock, rising from the water on the far side of a very narrow channel. On the edge of the channel, just beside the trail, there are several shady places where you can sit and eat your lunch and look out over the waters of an unnamed but very pretty pond.

Soon after you leave the picnic spot, the trail turns right, gradually descending. You are now passing through the thick, mature, mainly deciduous forest at the south end of Silent Lake. Throughout this section, the trail is always well back from the lake, but from time to time you catch a glimpse of water through the trees, always to your right. About 25 minutes after setting out from the lunch spot, you will encounter the red markers of a cross country ski trail that crosses the hiking trail here. Pay them no heed and stick to the blue markers.

From time to time over the next 1.5 to 2 kilometres, you may find the going difficult, because the understorey is very dense, and the trail is not well maintained—in places it is so overgrown that the track disappears. You must keep a very sharp lookout for trail markers. If you lose sight of the blue hiking icons, don't blunder on; stop, then retrace your steps to the last marker and look again.

The worst is over when you reach a point where the trail bears left and ascends to a narrow piece of ground between two ponds. It continues to rise to an elevated position overlooking the larger of the two ponds. Now the landscape is much more open, drier and dotted with pine trees, and the ground is rocky underfoot as you walk toward a very large cedar and black ash swamp at the pond's northern end. When you reach the swamp, you'll likely see a number of great blue herons and many nests in the tops of the dead trees. If you are there in late spring or summer, you may catch sight of one of the ospreys that have been nesting there for several years.

Now the trail follows the course of the stream as it descends a short distance through a rocky channel, into the main body of Silent Lake. When you reach the lakeside you can sit on the rocky shelf beside the stream and rest before the final stretch. Compared with the solitary splendour of the rest of the walk, you may be surprised to find the lookout quite busy—this is a favourite port of call for canoeists.

From here, you have about 3.5 kilometres still to go, but don't lose heart; this is the easiest bit of the hike. The path, passing through trees and over gently undulating terrain, first takes you south, then makes a wide curve to the west. After about 40 minutes, it brings you to a spot between two ponds. For the last 2 kilometres, you pass over almost level ground on a wide trail that brings you out onto the beach. You'll be hot and very tired, but flushed with pride, and if it's a hot day, I bet you'll summon up enough energy to crown your achievement with a swim!

Bon Echo Provincial Park

Trail Information: The park's four hiking trails cover 27 kilometres.

Abes and Essens Trail—9-kilometre loop, 4 hours, moderate. There are also 4- and 17-kilometre loops.

Access: On Highway 41, north of Highway 7, drive 10 kilometres north of Cloyne. The park entrance is on the right. All park users must pay a fee.

Map: Free information and trail guides are available at the Park Office.

Parking: For the Cliff Top and High Pines Trails, park at the Visitor Centre. For the Shield Trail and for Abes and Essens Trail, park near each trailhead.

The most striking thing about Bon Echo Provincial Park is Mazinaw Rock, a vast granite and gneiss cliff that towers 125 metres above the waters of Mazinaw Lake. It was born more than a billion years ago deep inside the earth's crust, when molten magma solidified and hardened. Many periods of upheaval over

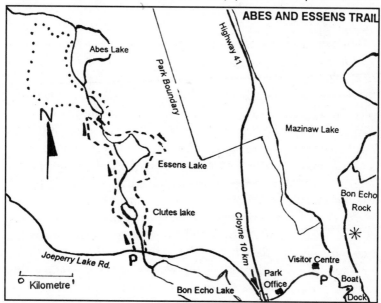

ABES AND ESSENS TRAIL

Abes Lake

Park Boundary

Highway 41

Mazinaw Lake

N

Essens Lake

Bon Echo Rock

Clutes lake

Cloyne 10 km

Joeperry Lake Rd.

P

Visitor Centre

P

Boat Dock

Park Office

Bon Echo Lake

Kilometre

Canoeing on Mazinaw lake 1936.
Source: National Archives of Canada, PA 1992971

hundreds of millions of years brought it closer to the surface, alongside a north-south fault line. Finally, tectonic movement and pressure along the fault pushed the east side upwards to form a sheer cliff, rising from a lake that is 100 metres deep.

For centuries, the rock has been a source of wonder and fascination. Even now, when you encounter it for the first time, its unexpectedness and immensity give you some sense of how it must have affected the first people who stumbled upon it many centuries ago. Hundreds of aboriginal pictographs on the rock's surface, painted in red ochre just above the waterline, confirm that this must indeed have been a much-revered place.

We don't know what the first European settlers felt about the rock: awe, almost certainly; reverence, probably not. For the early settler struggling to clear the land, searching among the ever-present rocks for elusive patches of soil, the sight of 125 metres of towering cliff might well have been a source of despair. Appreciation of its grandeur and stark beauty is perhaps easier for those who do not have to depend on the unyielding land for survival—a privilege of the affluent, and therefore a twentieth-century affair.

Its first recorded, non-Native admirer was Dr. Weston Price, who bought the rock in 1889 and built a hotel on the opposite shore. He named it Bon Echo on account of the clear echoes that rebound off the rock face. In 1910 the ownership passed to Flora McDonald Dennison, a Toronto businesswoman and women's suffrage activist, who was also a devotee of the poet Walt Whitman. The hotel became the hub of the Walt Whitman Society and, as a tangible testament of their esteem, the Whitman fans adorned—perhaps defaced—the surface of the rock with lines of his poetry carved in foot-high letters.

Flora's son, the playwright Merrill Dennison, took over the hotel in 1921. It continued to attract the rich—even providing a chauffeured Cadillac to carry visitors to and from the Kaladar railway station. The resort's cultural focus continued, however, and several members of the Group of Seven captured Mazinaw Rock and its glorious surroundings on canvas.

The resort's life came to an abrupt end in a fire in 1936. Twenty years later Dennison sold the land to the provincial government, and Bon Echo was recreated as a Provincial Park, to be enjoyed not just by the favoured few but by anyone who cared for the outdoor life and the natural environment. More land has been added over the years and today Bon Echo Provincial Park covers 6,644 hectares of forest and lakes.

With 500 drive-in campsites, good fishing and canoeing, safe, sandy beaches and hikes varying in length from 1.4 to 17 kilometres, it is an ideal place for a family vacation. The park staff runs a wide and varied series of programs: special activities for children, films and evening entertainment in the amphitheatre, nature programs and guided hikes. If you don't have your own boat, you can take an hour's cruise on Mazinaw Lake on the tourboat *Wanderer Too*, or, if you prefer to see the sights—particularly the pictographs —at your own pace, you can rent a canoe.

The 2-kilometre Cliff Top Trail is an absolute must. The *Mugwump* ferry boat takes you to a dock across the lake from which steps and a pathway lead you to the top of the rock. It's a fascinating journey that takes you past 700-year-old cedars clinging precariously to the rock face, rare mosses and lichens, and climbs up to observation decks that give wonderful views over the surrounding country.

Another short jaunt, the 1.4-kilometre High Pines Trail, takes you through the forest on the west shore of Mazinaw Lake and includes a splendid view of Mazinaw Rock.

If you are interested in history, you will find the Shield Trail fascinating. Starting out from the parking area on the Joeperry Lake Road just west of Highway 41, this 4.8-kilometre loop trail travels through rugged territory that was settled in the middle of the nineteenth century by hopeful homesteaders. The first part of the walk takes you along the Addington Road, a colonization road that ran from the Clare River to the Madawaska River. Built between 1854 and 1856, its purpose was partly to entice prospective homesteaders and partly to enable the logging companies to harvest valuable but otherwise inaccessible stands of timber.

When the road was finished, the blandishments to prospective settlers were hard to resist: "Free gift lots...excellent soil and climate ...abundance of water, heavy timber—almost always the best." The reality, as the rugged trail demonstrates, was very different: rock, thin soils and swamp. Many disillusioned settlers left.

For the logging companies it was a different story. Between 1860 and 1890 a logging bonanza brought some degree of stability for the homesteaders—extra work and a market for produce. However, as supplies of good timber waned, the lumber companies moved north, leaving a scarred landscape and small communities, which, deprived of their main source of subsistence, fell into decline.

After leaving the Addington Road, the trail swings west and then north toward Bon Echo Lake. It takes you along rocky ridges once covered with white pine that were 40 metres tall. Burned stumps along the way are legacies of the fires that frequently ravaged the logged areas. Near the lake the trail passes the site of an old log run, and then veers east to follow the line of the lake before rejoining the path back to the parking area.

Abes and Essens Trail

The Abes and Essens Trail is for those who like a challenge. There are three loops and you can decide to do one, two or all three. It's quite rugged so, if you want to do all 17 kilometres, you might prefer to take two days over it rather than try to tackle it all at once. There are several very pleasant wilderness campsites en route, but in the high season, you must book well ahead.

I have not done the full trek but I can thoroughly recommend the 9-kilometre Clutes–Essens Lake loop. It takes you through a varied landscape and is rugged and remote enough to give you a feel of the wilderness.

To get to the trailhead from the park office, follow signs to Joeperry Lake Road. The road passes underneath Highway 41. Drive about two kilometres and look for a parking area on the south side of the road. The entrance to the hike is on the other side of the road, close to a large map board.

The Clutes Lake Trail, marked with red disks, heads north through attractive mixed bush. Underfoot, the ground is rocky and moss-covered, strewn with tree roots and never, never flat. Good boots are a must. After about ten minutes, you pass a wet area on your right, then the trail veers left, taking you through pines and silver birch before coming out into more open country.

The path now passes along slightly elevated ground, with a river to your right. There are long vistas over the water meadows and to the north, where Clutes Lake soon comes into view. After you've been on the trail about 40 minutes, you start to walk down into a cool, shady valley. At the bottom, a jumble of rocks and trees lie in chaotic disarray along the river bed. A steepish climb takes you up the other side and, in about ten minutes, you find yourself walking over elevated ground on large shelves of rock.

Very soon you reach an intersection. The Clutes Lake Trail now heads right to cross over to the other side of the lake. However, you should keep left, following the yellow disks of the Essens Lake Trail. The path climbs very steadily until, after about 25 minutes, it brings you to a rocky vantage point. Moss covers the rocks underfoot, large boulders rise up behind, and through the tall trees in front of you, you catch your first glimpse of the blue waters of Essens Lake.

The trail continues to head north, still undulating, but making an overall descent, to bring you, after a further 20 minutes, to a very still pool. After skirting round the edge, you make a short, steep descent to an intersection. The orange disks of the third loop continue north. The yellow-marked Essens Lake Trail veers right, to cross a stream and start the homeward trek.

The crossing is made over huge rocky outcrops that rise from the wetlands north of Essens Lake. If you are hungry, there are several places to sit and have a snack, overlooking the water meadows that stretch out to the north. Water lilies, pickerel weed and flag irises flourish alongside dark patches of bog myrtle and juniper bushes; sombre conifers provide a dramatic backdrop.

(However, unless you are starving, I suggest waiting a little for lunch, as you have not yet reached the halfway point.)

Two hundred metres metres further along the trail, after passing a beaver dam, you arrive at the edge of Essens Lake. The path continues to hug the shoreline of this beautiful lake from a slightly elevated position which gives wonderful views of the tree-lined rocky shore. After several minutes, you'll pass a very pretty little island and walk through a stand of very tall pine. Here, (just about at the halfway point) there are several delightful spots for a lunch break, where you'll have a fine view over the water and the benefit of a breeze coming off the lake.

Just past the island, the trail turns sharp left and leaves the shoreline briefly, descending a rocky path, and then making a long right-hand bend. You'll notice that there is much more colour in the rocks on this side of the lake—many of the rocks are covered with green and grey lichens, and some rock surfaces have a distinct pink hue.

The trail continues to follow the shoreline, giving many spectacular views down the lake. Before long, you descend to a boardwalk that takes you over a large wet area. You begin a steep climb to high ground above the lake. A vigorous deciduous understorey and a thick carpet of ferns give the woods on this side of the lake a damper, more southern air.

About 45 minutes past the island lookout, you'll come to the first of two wilderness campsites. Set amidst trees high above the water, it has a commanding view north over the lake. After passing the second campsite, the path veers to the left, ascending to a ridge above marshy land.

When I did this walk, it seemed to take an inordinately long time (actually it was not much more than half an hour) to cover the distance between the two lakes. But, it was a very hot day, the mosquitoes were tiresome, and maybe I was getting tired. In any event, each time (three in all) that open water came into view, I optimistically thought that we had arrived at Clutes Lake, only to be disappointed!

Don't expect to find the intersection with the Clutes Lake Trail until you have reached a drier, rock-strewn area. Also, as you near the meeting of the trails, there is a bit of confused signage—trail markers seem to point in all directions. If you keep to the left and follow the yellow signs down a hill, you'll quickly reach the end of Clutes Lake and pick up the red trail markers.

The path follows the treed shoreline south along the east side of Clutes Lake. The terrain is flat and the going easy. After about 40 minutes, you reach the park road at a point slightly east of the parking lot.

Other Central Cottage Country Trails

Trails in Muskoka

Over the past few years, the Muskoka Recreational Trails Council has been making a concerted effort to create trails and promote hiking. The task is not easy, given that there are no vast tracts of publicly owned, undeveloped lands within the Central Muskoka area. However, the council has done a great job; it has managed to establish a number of trails and has produced a detailed, 28-page brochure that lists and describes all the possible trails. Among the list of 32 trails are some that are primarily for hikers and others that are primarily for cross country skiers or cyclists. Many of the trails sound as if they are ideal for beginners: the lengths vary, but most of the hiking trails seem to be between 1 and 8 kilometres in length and travel over relatively easy terrain. Some are linear; some are loops. I have not been able to get around many of them; however, the ones mentioned below are definitely worth knowing about. To obtain the Muskoka Trails brochure, call (705) 645-8121.

Torrance Barrens Conservation Reserve is a 1990-hectare wilderness area accessible from Muskoka Road 13, 7 kilometres south of Torrance (just off Highway 169, south of Bala). Barren rock ridges in places sparsely treed with oak, pine and ash are interspersed with low wetlands. A network of 10 kilometres of hiking trails—three loops in all—takes the hiker around ponds, through wetlands and over rock. The trails, which are marked with stone cairns and metal signs, are not difficult to follow, and walkways, laid over some boggy areas, make the going easier.

The Bracebridge Management Resource Centre (MNR) is located between Highway 11 and the North Muskoka River, on the east side of the highway, 2.4 kilometres north of the High Falls Bridge. The network of trails within its 607 hectares has been designed for cross country skiers. During the rest of the year, they serve very nicely as hiking trails.

A large map showing the trails is displayed in the car park. Altogether there are 8 kilometres of connecting loops of varying

An enigmatic group in the Torrance Barrens.
Source: Archives of Ontario, C7 16980

degrees of ruggedness. So, with a bit of planning, you can devise an interesting and varied hike of about 5 kilometres that will take you along the river—meandering slowly and gently at this point—and through hardwood forest. The best time of year to hike is the fall, when the hardwood trees lining both sides of the river are aflame with colour.

You'll see the North Muskoka River in an entirely different mood if you hike to Wilson's Falls. Although the falls is only 2 kilometres north of the centre of Bracebridge, the landscape has an astonishingly wild and primitive feel to it. An easy trail leads alongside the river to the bottom of the falls, where the North Muskoka plunges over a 12.5-metre cliff. A more rugged path climbs up through pines and over rocky outcrops to the top. It's a splendid sight at any time, but if you happen to be there in early spring, you'll see a white wall of water, 100 metres wide, thundering down the rocks. A footbridge at the bottom of the falls lets you cross the river to look at the falls from a different perspective. From this side you can also walk up to a picnic area close to the river at the top of the falls.

Grandview Inn and Deerhurst Resort are large resorts near Huntsville. Hiking trails are among their many attractions. Non-guests are welcome to hike the trails, so, if you fancy a taste of resort living while you are hiking, Grandview Inn and Deerhurst are very handy for both Algonquin and Arrowhead.

Another resort that has its own hiking trails is Rocky Crest on Lake Joseph. Located on 130 hectares of its own land just east of Highway 69 on Hamer Bay Road, its 8 kilometres of cross country ski trails are excellent for hiking. The trails, which are moderately rugged, run largely through mature forest and afford some wonderful views over Lake Joseph. Rocky Crest, incidentally, is quite handily placed for exploring Massasauga Provincial Park.

Grandview and Rocky Crest have recently become part of ClubLink Resorts, Muskoka, a golf-oriented organization. At the present time, the hiking trails are intact, but at some stage in the future, as new greens and fairways encroach, some of them are bound to disappear. For information call 1-800-461-4454.

Trails in Haliburton

Northwest of the town of Haliburton, on County Road 7 (Kennisis Lake Road), the Haliburton Forest and Wild Life Reserve Ltd. stretches over 21,000 hectares of glorious countryside—rolling hardwood forest, wetland, rivers and 50 lakes. Within the boundary of this privately owned reserve, there are upwards of 300 kilometres of trails. While they have been primarily designed for mountain biking (snowmobiling in winter) many of them make very good hiking trails. They form a huge and complex network, so you should buy the trail map, study it and decide where to go. The terrain varies from flat to very rugged, and, as cars are allowed along a number of the wider trails (old logging roads), groups with two cars should be able to make some creative, car-ferrying, loop hikes. The further into the reserve you go, the wilder it gets.

I have only hiked there for a couple of days, so my knowledge is very limited. It was August and the weather was a bit unsettled, so maybe that is why we didn't encounter a single bicycle! In any case, the area is so huge that I don't think that bicycles would pose a problem. The walking was very lovely but perhaps somewhat lacking in panoramic views. Most of the time we were in tall forest or walking along the edge of beautiful, utterly deserted lakes. The daily charge to use the trails is $10 per person. For more information call (705) 754-2198.

In addition to bicycling and hiking, you can fish, canoe, take part in the many outdoor education programs and even visit a resident wolf pack. For people who want to stay, there is a choice of private housekeeping units and lodge accommodation. Campsites are mostly leased on a yearly basis, but there are a few short-stay sites. When I visited, I stayed at Meadow Wood, a delightful B&B a few kilometres south of the reserve. Pam and Joe Smith make their guests very welcome and serve a wonderful breakfast that sets you up for the day! For more information call (705) 754-1234.

Nineteen kilometres northeast of Haliburton, off County Road 19, at the end of Drag Lake, you'll find the Domain of Killien. This very small, very exclusive resort, sits on 2,100 hectares of private land. It is not glossy; there is no radio or television, but you can play tennis, canoe, sail or swim. And you can hike. Winding through forests, along the shores of tiny lakes and over huge outcrops of rock, 28 kilometres of hiking trails pass through some of the finest hiking country I have seen on the Shield. There is just one snag— the trails are only open to residents!

I think you need a very special occasion to go there. My excuse was a BIG birthday, and it was worth it. One day we walked 16 rugged kilometres, through a breathtakingly beautiful landscape and saw not a single soul. Then we topped the whole thing off with a superb dinner, overlooking a tranquil lake—my idea of bliss. If you think you might want to indulge in a unique hiking experience you can find out more by calling (705) 457-1556.

Ganaraska Trail

The Ganaraska Trail runs between Port Hope and Glen Huron. The northern and southern parts of the trail pass through rolling farmland and woods, and along country roads. Connecting these two parts, the Wilderness Section of the Ganaraska Trail winds for 65.5 kilometres, between Moore Falls, on Gull Lake in the east corner of Haliburton County, and Sadowa, near the western edge of Victoria County. It passes through some of the wildest and most rugged country on the southern part of the Canadian Shield. The trail, marked only by intermittently placed white blazes, is very difficult to follow, very demanding, and suitable only for very fit and experienced hikers. For more information, contact the Ganaraska Hiking Trail Association, Box 693, Orillia, ON L3V 6K7.

Hastings Heritage Trail

When it was started in 1873, the Central Ontario Railway was meant to run from Trenton, through Hastings County, to link with the Ottawa Arnprior and Parry Sound Railway near Whitney. In addition to serving the lumber industry, the COR played a crucial part in transporting iron ore after that mineral was discovered in the hills south of Bancroft. Although the railway never made it to Whitney —it terminated at Lake St. Peter—it was an important transportation route for both freight and passengers, and it played a major part in opening up central and north Hastings. It had a pretty long life—it wasn't formally abandoned until 1982. In 1993, the 156-kilometre stretch of railbed between Glen Ross and Lake St. Peter became a multi-use recreational trail, the Hastings Heritage Trail.

Obviously, there are opportunities to walk any number of sections along the way. In *Hiking Ontario's Heartland*, Shirley Teasdale recommends the 6-kilometre stretch between Graphite and Hybla, just to the north of Bancroft, on the east side of Highway 62. As with all the linear trails, this walk is easier if your group has two cars.

If you are here in summer and feel like a bit more hiking, drive north on Highways 62 and 127 to Lake St. Peter, where there is a small provincial park, a very pleasant 5-kilometre hiking trail and good swimming from a delightful sandy beach.

There are excellent drive-in campsites at Arrowhead, Bon Echo and Silent Lake Provincial Parks. A wide variety of accommodations —resorts, lodges, motels and B&Bs—can be found throughout Central Cottage Country. See page 149 for useful contact numbers.

Central Cottage Country

Rideau Valley

Between Kingston and Brockville, there lies a narrow band of the Canadian Shield—the Frontenac Axis—which continues southeast into the Adirondack region of New York State. Its crossing of the St. Lawrence River is marked by a rocky archipelago, the Thousand Islands, one of the best-known tourist attractions in the country. However, the main part of the Frontenac Axis lies north of the river, running through the counties of Frontenac, Leeds and Grenville, and Lanark.

This axis forms a rugged and sometimes wild landscape of wooded hills, bare rocky ridges and hundreds of interconnected lakes and streams. Here, in a rough rectangle bounded by Kingston, Brockville, Perth and the hamlet of Sharbot Lake, you will find some of the best hiking in Cottage Country. The terrain is wonderful to walk over, but, as you'll say to yourself time and time again, hard to live off!

With good land in short supply, only the first wave of immigrants was lucky enough to receive land amenable to agriculture. The majority had to make do with less fertile land, and, as time went on and the surveyors pressed ever northward, some homesteaders found themselves in possession of land deemed, even by the men who surveyed it, as totally unsuitable for settlement.

The story of the struggles of the European immigrants is a familiar one: settlers arriving in the early 1800s to take on, sight unseen, two hundred acres of rock and forest, with only the odd pocket of arable soil. The labour of clearing the land was back-breaking, and the progress painfully slow. But perhaps one of the most daunting aspects of life in the bush was the isolation. Any journey, whether to buy supplies, transport logs, or simply to visit a neighbour, involved a laborious and sometimes dangerous foray into near-trackless wilderness. Many gave up the struggle, but some stubbornly persisted.

Had it not been for the War of 1812, their hardship and isolation might have continued much longer than it did. But the war had clearly pinpointed the vulnerability of the St. Lawrence River as a supply route. Fearing another invasion, the Canadian and British governments initiated an exhaustive search for an alternate, safer route, well out of reach of the potentially hostile southern neighbour. After much cogitation, the governments decided to construct a canal from the mouth of the Rideau River down to Kingston.

Masterminded by Colonel John By, the canal was completed in 1832, and although its military importance was debatable, its commercial success was immediate. It had a huge impact on the areas close to the waterway. Travel, hitherto a difficult and hazardous process, suddenly became manageable. For fledgling logging companies, the canal eased the task of getting logs from bush to sawmill. In a short time, logging became not only an important commercial operation but also a welcome supplementary source of income for isolated homesteaders—they were able to make agreements to supply cut lumber to large logging companies. Later in the century, similar agreements were made between settlers and mining companies. (On the southern edge of the Shield, deposits of mica—a heat-resistant crystalline mineral used for panels in stoves, safety glasses, electrical insulation and lubrication—were common, and many settlers dug shafts on their land and extracted the mineral with pick and shovel.) In time, both logging and mining companies extended the network of bush roads, making travel and commerce easier, even for those living far from the waterway.

Small communities grew up in the most remote places. Nearer to the canal, mill sites proliferated, but, between 1840 and the end of the century, as logging and mining operations expanded, bustling ports developed on the water. Some, it must be said, had but a short life: by the early years of the twentieth century, as timber supplies gave out and changing technology reduced the need for mica, the commercial importance of the canal waned and, bereft of their economic underpinnings, the waterside communities began to decline.

The canal was saved from oblivion largely by the beauty of its surrounding landscape; it took on a new life as a recreational waterway. Cottages and hotels replaced the sawmills, and the surviving communities traded their nineteenth-century industrial bustle for a more modest and tranquil existence as tourist centres.

Today, a network of reasonable roads takes you through terrain that was virtually impassable a hundred years ago. However, if you want to get the true flavour of the Canadian Shield, you will not neglect the waterways, and you should make some expeditions on foot.

Happily, there is a trail that will take you all the way from

Rideau Valley

Bedford Mills during its heyday as a thriving milling town.

Source: Janet Tett/Miles, Christian Barber

Kingston to Ottawa. The Rideau Trail (see page 147) is a 387-kilo-metre, cleared and marked hiking trail that roughly follows the route of the Rideau Canal. It makes travel on foot a relatively simple matter.

Along the section of the Rideau Trail that passes through Shield country, two provincial parks and two conservation areas offer some

spectacular hiking. Murphys Point Provincial Park on Big Rideau Lake, and Foley Mountain Conservation Area on Upper Rideau Lake front directly onto the Rideau Canal. Frontenac Provincial Park and Gould Lake Conservation Area lie on rugged, inhospitable land just to the south. The choices they offer are many—from an easy stroll alongside a sandy beach to a scramble over perpendicular rocks in what feels like the wildest wilderness. If you don't know this part of Cottage Country, it's time to discover it!

Frontenac Provincial Park

Trail Information: The network of park trails covers 170 kilometres.

Kingsford Dam Loop—11-kilometre loop, 5 hours, moderate

Big Salmon Lake Loop—19-kilometre loop, 7-8 hours, strenuous

Slide Lake Loop—14 kilometres, 7 hours, strenuous

Access: From Highway 401, exit north onto County Road 9 (exit #613). County Road 9 ends when it meets Rutledge Road. Turn left onto Rutledge Road and after about 2 kilometres, turn right, following the signs to Frontenac Provincial Park through Sydenham. After travelling north along Bedford Road for about 10 kilometres, look out for a sign to Frontenac Provincial Park on your right. The park entrance is about 2 kilometres along Salmon Lake Road. All park users must pay a fee.

Map: A free information guide is available at the Trail Centre. I recommend that you buy the excellent topographical map of the park.

Parking: Near the start of each trail.

Before I started research for this book, I had no idea that Frontenac Provincial Park existed. Now that I have begun to explore its trails, it has become one of my favourite places to hike in Ontario. It sprawls over about 70 square kilometres of rugged terrain, and it's one of the few places where I've felt that hiking comes at the very top of the list of activities. There is no drive-in camping; to move around the park, you have to be in a boat or on foot, and if you are on foot, there is a network of 170 kilometres of trail to take you to every corner of the park.

There are 48 water's-edge campsites—each with tent pad, shared privy and a glorious view. Day users are also very welcome, and two short hiking trails, very near the Trail Centre at Otter Lake, will give you an immediate and delightful introduction to the park and its scenery. However, if you are feeling more adventurous, you will find a number of the longer, more-challenging trails are readily accessible. My excursions have always been on a daily basis, yet I have managed to complete one of the longest loops and still get back to my B&B in time for dinner.

So, what makes Frontenac so special?

To begin with, the park's geology has produced three separate environmental zones, each with a distinct landscape and mixture of flora and fauna. In the most northern part, where the bedrock is mostly marble, a forest of tall deciduous trees such as white ash, sugar maple, butternut and shagbark hickory thrive in the relatively deep soils of a rolling landscape. Beneath the shady canopy, you can find some of Ontario's rarest ferns and orchids. South of here, a band of granitic gneiss forms the bedrock of a landscape of more open ridges and wooded valleys covered with white pine, birch, beech, oak and maple. The most southern region of the park has a hard, gneiss and diorite bedrock, which has produced a rugged, inhospitable landscape of rocky outcrops, shallow ponds, bogs and many bare, burned-over ridges—the legacy of three major fires.

And then there is Frontenac's rich human history. For many years the park area was home to a thriving, closely-knit community largely made up of farming families, loggers and miners. Even though there is little evidence of their presence today, time and again the hiker will suddenly encounter a poignant remnant of a vanished age—flakes of mica gleaming through fallen leaves, an old gatepost, or a collapsed barn building. Nothing startling or dramatic, just a persistent reminder that, for 150 years, the land that now appears so natural, so untouched, was cleared, farmed, logged, mined, lived on and played on, and that it has been profoundly and irrevocably shaped and altered by its human tenancy.

The three loops described here take you to each of the park's three zones. The first is an 11-kilometre walk. It leads you on an exploration of the north end of the park, through mature hardwood forests, past an abandoned mica mine, across a gorge and around the shores of two pristine lakes. The second is a truly spectacular walk round Big Salmon Lake. It is a long haul, 19 kilometres in all, but it takes you through wonderfully varied terrain and visits many marvellous viewpoints. The third, Slide Lake Loop, on the south boundary of the park (my favourite walk) is part of the Rideau Trail.

At 14 kilometres, it's not the longest, but it's the most rugged by far, and the views are spectacular.

Kingsford Dam Loop via Lynch Lake and Clearwater Lake

This trail starts at the park's north entrance. Pick up a park permit at the Trail Centre, then leave the park and head north on Bedford Road. After about 4.7 kilometres, when the main road veers left toward Verona, keep straight on, along the side road (Bedford Road), heading north. After a further 9 kilometres, look for an even smaller road on your right. Turn right to travel east along this road. After about 1 kilometre you'll pass a house on the right and, shortly thereafter, turn right, onto a cottage road. Keep to the left branch and, after a couple of hundred metres, you will arrive at a small parking area at Kingsford Dam.

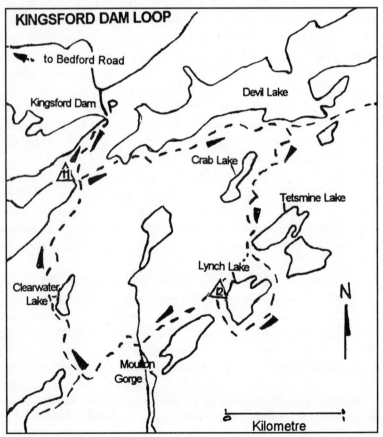

KINGSFORD DAM LOOP

to Bedford Road

Kingsford Dam P

Devil Lake

Crab Lake

Tetsmine Lake

Lynch Lake

Clearwater Lake

Moulton Gorge

N

Kilometre

The present dam was built in the 1940s to control water levels in Kinsgford Lake, but there has been a dam on or near this site for 150 years. For many years this was a crucial way-station for logs on their tortuous journey from Big Salmon Lake via Moulton Gorge, Birch, Kingsford and Devil Lakes to Bedford Mills.

On the other side of the footbridge, a wide path, which in the mid-nineteenth century led to two farms, heads south through tall mature trees. Along the route there are some spectacular white birch. After about 600 metres, the trail divides. Take the left fork, signposted to Moulton and Tetsmine Lakes. The trail continues over gently rolling terrain, through a tall deciduous forest that forms a shady canopy. In spring, the forest floor is carpeted with hepaticas, Dutchman's breeches, and trout lilies. Later, particularly where it's damp, lush ferns flourish alongside wood lily and cardinal flower.

After almost 2 kilometres, you come upon the remains of a mica mine on the right side of the trail. This was one of the Crab Lake Mines, which flourished between 1880 and 1949. The cavity is now filled with water and fenced off, but mica chips gleam through the forest-floor debris all around the site. Beyond the mine, the path descends quite steeply and, through the trees, you catch a glimpse of Devil Lake. After a few minutes, when the trail divides, keep right, toward Tetsmine Lake.

You are walking along a low ridge, through bush, on what was probably an old mining road. The terrain becomes somewhat rockier and, after about ten minutes, you reach a huge rock outcrop. Trees seem to sprout from the top, mosses and ferns cloak its sides, and numerous striations confirm that it has been scoured by a glacier. Cracks and fallen boulders show that erosion continues to take its toll.

Soon, the path approaches a small lake. The trail takes you over some logs, then veers right to skirt the lake, taking you at a slightly elevated level, through rocky, grassy, scrubby terrain where staghorn sumac predominate. A small cairn helps you to keep to the right path. Then, after a few minutes, you descend into a different world. Suddenly you are among large trees in a wet, green hollow. Ferns are everywhere and, on the fallen trees that lie half-submerged in shallow pools of water, they blend with mosses and grasses to form exquisite bog gardens.

You leave the cool, damp place as abruptly as you entered it, emerging into a sunny wetland with a boardwalk to keep you above the marsh. A loud chorus of frogs will perhaps serenade you as you pass. The trail continues over dry, grassy, rock-strewn terrain

Rideau Valley

for another 300 metres or so, before re-entering trees just as you approach Tetsmine Lake. (You will probably have been on the trail for about two hours and you are almost at the halfway point.) The lake is just visible on your left. The path crosses an old beaver dam and continues round the end of the lake.

When the trail forks, keep right, on the trail to Little Clear Lake. After a few minutes, the trail divides again. Here, you can take either branch. The left branch is more direct and takes you around the north end of Lynch Lake; the right branch takes you south, toward Little Clear Lake, before veering right to take you around the south and west sides of Lynch Lake. The longer route—the one I chose—takes you past campsite 12, which, if it is not occupied, is a great place for a rest.

The trail approaches Lynch Lake, at first over rocky terrain, but it soon enters lovely woods, mostly deciduous, with conifers near the water. Be sure to keep on the trail heading for campsite 12, which you should reach about 40 minutes after Tetsmine Lake. Picnic tables at the lakeside and a splendid view over the tree-ringed lake make this a perfect place for lunch.

Back on the trail, you'll reach a T-junction after about ten minutes. Turn left, toward campsite 11. Soon you meet open country and find yourself in an overgrown, sun-drenched meadow, studded with flowers. As you pass, Jacob's ladder, yellow and white yarrow and ranunculus vie with each other for your attention.

When the trail takes you back into trees, you'll notice that there is quite a steep-sided gorge to your right. A large mica mine, one of the biggest in Ontario, used to operate just to the north of the trail. Many shafts were dug hereabouts, the deepest one, 30 metres. All the mine buildings are long gone but, on the north ridge of the ravine, the old steam boiler still remains. It's not visible from the trail, but you can tell when you are pretty near the mine by the tell-tale flakes of mica gleaming underfoot.

The trail makes a steep descent to a very large marsh covered with a sea of bulrushes. The path makes a sharp turn, almost doubling back on itself, before heading north along the eastern edge of Moulton Gorge. The gorge, which cuts through a series of ridges, follows a geological fault line. In the nineteenth century this fortuitous breach in the bedrock was effectively exploited by the logging companies. The stream running through the centre of the gorge is a mere trickle now, so it's hard to imagine how it must have looked when it was part of a major water route used to move logs from Big Salmon Lake to Bedford Mills. Dams were needed to

The Tett Mine, ca 1905.
Source Janet Tett/Miles, Christian Barber

build up a sufficient head of water to flush the logs into the gorge and along a chute.

As you approach the north end of the gorge, you'll see the large flat rocks that were once part of the log chute and you'll need to do a bit of rock scrambling to reach the small bridge to take you across. On the other side, when the trail divides, take the right branch, signposted to campsites 8 and 11 and Kingsford Dam.

Soon the trail climbs into much rockier terrain and briefly becomes a little more tricky to negotiate. It makes a sharp left turn and heads southwest along a ridge. The view to the left, over the rocky north end of Moulton Gorge, is spectacular. After about 350 metres the trail veers right, and very soon you pass the trail leading to campsite 8.

The landscape becomes rockier and hillocky, with very little level ground, and the path threads its way through large boulders. After about 15 minutes, the tops of the trees surrounding

Rideau Valley

Clearwater Lake come into view, then the lake itself. You turn left to skirt the lake just before you get to its south end, which is shallow and rather marshy. Along its east shore, however, vertical cliffs plunge dramatically into the water, and on its west side, enormous rounded rocks slope downwards, some steeply, some gently. If it's a hot day, it will be a sight that makes you crave for a swim. Happily, with a very little effort, it's possible to make your way down a very large rock on the west side to a perfect swimming place. Just follow the trail for a few minutes around the lake, then cross though the bush at a point opposite the largest rock. When you get to the top, you'll see that there is an easy way down. There's a flattish ledge close to the water where you can slip in and out with ease.

My swim in Clearwater Lake was one of the best of my life. It was a very still, hot day, but by afternoon there was not much sun, so the grey rocks reflected in the lake gave it a solemn, almost mysterious air. A lone, male loon patrolling the centre of the lake watched us closely, then started to circle and dive, each time breaking the surface nearer and nearer to where we were swimming. It was as if he welcomed the company!

After Clearwater Lake, you walk through very pleasant, high, rather open country for about 15 minutes, before descending one more time into moist, deciduous woods. You stay in woods for the rest of the walk. When you reach the sign for campsite 11, you rejoin your original path to retrace your steps back to Kingsford Dam.

Big Salmon Lake Loop

Leave your car at the last parking area (the one closest to the lake) on Big Salmon Lake Road. From the picnic area, take the trail (marked with a blue diamond-shaped hiking icon) that leads along the south shore of the lake on a slightly elevated path. A few trees stand between you and the water, but you get really good views over the lake to the rocky north shore. After a few minutes, the wider Corridor Trail, coming from the Trail Centre, enters from the right. You continue to follow the line of the lake, still climbing gently through wooded terrain. After about 20 minutes you pass a lovely pond, covered with water lilies and bordered by rocks and grasses.

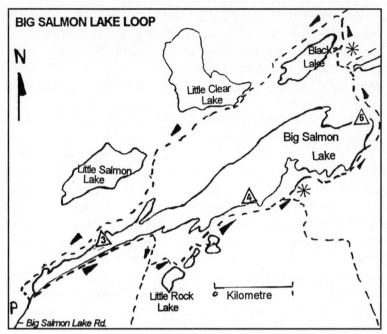

BIG SALMON LAKE LOOP

N

Little Clear Lake

Black Lake

Little Salmon Lake

Big Salmon Lake

⑥

④

⑤

③

Little Rock Lake

Kilometre

P

Big Salmon Lake Rd.

For the next 30 minutes, the trail passes through varied, undulating terrain, sometimes through thick woods, sometimes through scrub, with frequent beautiful views over the lake. After you have been walking for about 50 minutes, the path turns away from the lake and heads south, bringing you to a high, dry, rocky, open area. Climb up one of the large rock outcrops to get a wonderful view over the lake to the wooded ridge beyond.

After another five minutes the path forks. Take the left fork, signposted to campsites 4 and 5. It leads you down through cool, deciduous woods, before emerging into more open country. A boardwalk takes you over a marshy area and, after about ten minutes, you find yourself on much drier terrain, overlooking a very pretty lake on your right, most aptly called Little Rock Lake.

Soon the trail turns to head back toward Big Salmon Lake, leaving the open, rocky landscape and entering woods once again. If you are there in July, you'll see lots of bunchberry, but keep a lookout too for large patches of wonderfully sweet wild strawberries.

You reach the shore of Big Salmon Lake about 20 minutes after leaving Little Rock Lake. If campsite 4 is not in use, go down the water's edge. Wind soughing through the tall trees, and the intense blue of the calm water lend a magical touch to the spot, whatever the time of year.

Rideau Valley

Beyond the campsite, the trail heads east. It ascends a little as it moves back from the lake and quickly brings you to more open, sparsely treed, higher, drier terrain. After about 15 minutes, when you come to a fork, take the left path. You are walking northeast over rocky terrain, among large clumps of juniper and stands of staghorn sumac. There is very little shade, and the last time I was there—a brilliantly sunny Thanksgiving weekend—numerous garter snakes were enjoying the last rays of warm sun.

As you walk over this high plateau, you get great views both to the north and southeast. After two or three minutes, Big Salmon Lake comes into view, and the trail descends gradually. The path veers right just before it reaches the water, to take you in an easterly direction, roughly following the shoreline. After a few minutes, you find yourself very close to the water's edge, directly opposite some small rocky islands just out from the shore.

This is a lovely spot. Pine trees line the rocky shore, and the little islands are adorned with small pines, mosses, cranberry and blueberry bushes. Where the rock is bare, bold striations left by the glacier stand out sharply on the surface.

The path continues for a little along the shoreline, crosses the portage route to Labelle Lake, and then starts to rise a little, emerging from the trees once again, into more open country. Take a backward glance here to get a magnificent view back over Big Salmon Lake. As the trail veers gradually round to the north, it starts to descend, passing through hardwoods. Then, after a few minutes, it brings you down into a dramatic, rocky gorge. Very large trees rise from the bottom of the gorge, and a bridge takes you over a little stream.

The path to campsite 5 leads off to the left. This is the eastern end of the lake; you have covered about 8 kilometres, so you are still a little short of the halfway point. Although you will probably have been on the trail for two and a half to three hours, unless you are really hungry and in need of a rest (and this not a great spot to stop) you are better to press on for another 30 minutes.

After a steep ascent up the other side of the gorge, you emerge again into more open country. The path takes you over rocky terrain and, after a few minutes, passes a small, marshy lake. Junipers line your route, and the rocky outcrops become even larger and more spectacular until, after about five minutes, you pass a pond on your left that is completely surrounded by huge outcrops of rock. In the fall it's a wonderfully colourful scene—the blue-green of the juniper and the deeper greens of scattered cedar and pine set against the grey background of the rocks. Blazing out amongst the sombre colours are brilliant patches of orange and yellow hawk-weed and purple-spotted knapweed.

A few minutes past the pond, you descend back into immature hardwoods and, a couple of minutes later, as Black Lake comes into view ahead, you come to a fork in the trail. The trail on the right goes down to campsite 13. Keep left, following the path to Black Lake. You make a rocky ascent to a small cairn and, just beyond, you'll find a perfect spot for lunch, on the top of an enormous whale-backed rock, overlooking a small pond. There are wonderful views over the countryside to the north.

Back on the route to Black Lake, the trail descends to an old beaver meadow. Tree stumps remain, but the wetland has long ago dried up. The trail skirts round the edge to a little log bridge that crosses over what was obviously once the site of the beaver dam. Shortly after, the portage to Black Lake goes off to the left, while the Big Salmon Lake trail takes you right. The path passes some rocky outcrops and brings you to a log bridge across the stream that flows east from Black Lake. It's a wild, chaotic scene—many downed trees amongst a jumble of rocks.

The ground rises a little after the bridge, and soon you will begin to notice that the hardwood trees are getting larger. About ten minutes past the bridge, you encounter an enormous twin-trunked maple. About three times larger than any of the other trees, it is an obvious survivor of the old forest.

A couple of minutes later, the path veers sharply to the left to join a wide trail. This is the start of the homeward stretch. You are walking on Hardwood Bay Road, an old settlement road that used to link the park area to the settlements along the Perth Road. Although not much remains to recall the presence of the people who lived here, for the next 3.5 kilometres you will follow in the footsteps of the farming families, loggers and miners who, over a period of more than a hundred years, lived, worked and sometimes died, in this small corner of Canada.

After about ten minutes, you'll reach the portage connecting Black Lake and Bear Lake. It's hard to believe that this was once the home of an active little community. There is not much left: a fast-collapsing barn and a few foundations of farm buildings. Further along the trail, you pass gate posts built by one of the farmers, Wellington Green, and an old truck abandoned by contractors building a cottage road. Of the cottages that once stood on the shores of Little Clear Lake in the 1950s and 1960s, nothing

The McComish Farm, overlooking Black Lake, ca 1930.
Four generations of the McComish family lived and farmed
on Black Lake for 91 years.
Source: Ella McComish, Christian Barber

remains. The trail, however, gives you very pretty views across the waters of Little Clear Lake and, if you feel in need of a rest at this point, a grassy bank by the lake beckons invitingly.

About half an hour after reaching Little Clear Lake you reach an intersection. Take the left fork, signed to Big Salmon Lake, campsite 3 and the Trail Centre. After ten minutes or so, you reach an elevated, rocky ridge with a very tall pine standing on the top. A steep descent from it takes you down into a very pretty ravine where you cross a fast-flowing, rock-strewn stream on a bridge made out of two half-logs.

A short ascent then brings you into a mature hardwood forest. The trees are very large here, forming a high canopy that allows enough light to support a vigorous understorey of maple. After 15 minutes you reach the short path that leads down to campsite 3, which, if it is empty, is a perfect place for a final rest: a shady, tranquil spot overlooking the lake and the rocky south shore. And if you feel tired, take heart—you have only 40 minutes more to go.

From the campsite, the path follows the line of the lake, about 20 metres in from the shore. After about ten minutes you cross the portage to Little Salmon Lake and, immediately afterwards, a boardwalk takes you over a marshy inlet. After skirting round the remains of old beaver dams, the trail makes a short ascent to more open, rocky terrain. You pass a beautiful lily pond bordered by large rocks, and soon the path starts to descend again. When you come to a fork, keep left. The trail brings you round the end of the lake and, with another boardwalk to take you easily over the marshy bits, in less than ten minutes you are back at your starting place, probably very somewhat weary but mightily pleased with your achievements!

Slide Lake Loop

T his walk begins on the east side of the park, where the Rideau Trail emerges onto the Perth Road (County Road 10). The point of entry is quite difficult to find. If you are travelling north on County Road 10, look for an orange triangle on the fence on the west side of the road, at a point 2.5 kilometres past the turn-off to Opinicon–Chaffey's Locks. A few metres further on you'll see a small parking space marked "Parking for Rideau Trail." If you are travelling south on County Road 10, you'll find the space 5.3 kilometres past the Buck Lake sign.

Walk a few metres into the bush from the parking area to pick up the Rideau Trail, which runs roughly parallel to the road at this point. It veers left to ascend a small, rocky outcrop, and then follows the road again for a few metres before heading west into the bush. It's well blazed and a little rocky underfoot, but not difficult. After about half an hour, the trail skirts round a large beaver pond and enters cool, shady, more mature woods. The path takes a pleasant, undulating course through the woods, bringing you, after about 20 minutes, to a stile. A notice tells you that this is the park boundary. Shortly after, a sign pointing to the right bears the word "view." Be sure not to miss it. A short, rocky ascent brings you to wonderful lookout over Buck Lake.

There is no need to retrace your steps; blazes lead you down through a steep, rocky gully to flatter terrain and, after a couple of minutes, bring you out of the woods into a huge meadow. Here you'll see a large sign and a map of the Slide Lake Loop. You are

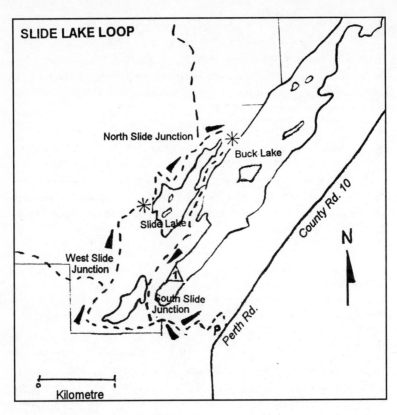

SLIDE LAKE LOOP

North Slide Junction

Buck Lake

County Rd. 10

N

Slide Lake

West Slide
Junction

1

South Slide
Junction

Perth Rd.

P

0   1
Kilometre

now at South Slide Junction and at this point, you have probably been walking for about an hour.

The loop is 8.7 kilometres, and the direction you decide to travel is entirely a matter of personal preference. I have done it both ways and prefer to go round in a clockwise direction—it takes you over the less-attractive parts of the walk near the start and, when you get to Slide Lake, the views are more dramatic. But either way, it's a fascinating and challenging journey.

To take the clockwise route, follow the orange triangles of the Rideau Trail west, across the meadow and along a wide path that was once a wagon trail. The landscape, even now, is thoroughly bucolic—small pine and juniper scattered throughout the meadow, a lake just visible through the trees on your left. In summer, cattle graze in the meadow on the other side of a split-rail fence.

After about ten minutes, you'll follow the trail around the edge of a very large beaver pond and then re-enter the cover of very tall, mature trees. The terrain becomes more rocky, and soon you reach a very large rocky outcrop. Be careful here: don't go up the rocks; instead, look for cairns and blazes that take you to the left. Very soon, you pass between an enormous outcrop on your left and a swamp on your right.

Thirty to forty minutes after leaving South Slide Junction, you reach West Slide Junction. Turn north here to start the west side of the loop. The path quickly becomes drier, very rocky and anything but flat! (The trail is now marked by both a blue triangle and a blue diamond with a white hiking icon.) After a few minutes you ascend some rocks and get a very good view of a large beaver meadow below. A little further on, you reach a sign pointing right to "The Overlook." Actually it's a bit of a misnomer; there are wonderfully long views on all sides, but it doesnt actually overlook anything.

By now the terrain is very rocky and much more open, with clumps of juniper and pine dotting the landscape. The trail is well blazed, but you do have to keep a sharp eye open. Don't go on unless you can see the next blaze. The going is rugged and, as you continue what seems to be an endless series of ascents and descents you may begin to wonder where on earth Slide Lake has got to. Don't lose heart. About an hour, (approximately 2 kilometres) after West Slide Junction, you climb to the top of an enormous rock and there it is below you, stretching out to the north—blue, silent and still. Along its western shores, great rocks plunge straight into the water. On the east side, a canopy of green spreads out as far as the eye can see. It's a lovely sight. Others have thought so, too. Just past your first sighting of the lake, when you toil to the top of an even higher rock, you'll see a sign bearing the words, "a bloody great rock by a bonnie wee loch"—what more needs to be said?

From here you travel along the western shore, high above the lake, along the top of great whale-backed rocks, the views getting better and better all the time. You've probably been on the trail for about two and a half hours by now and may be in need of a rest. There are some wonderful, airy places to stop along this stretch. If it's hot and you want to swim as well as eat, there is a perfect spot just about opposite the second of two small islands, where you can descend quite easily to a shaded, grass-covered, rocky ledge just above the water. Here, the water is deep, and the rock shelf gives easy entry. What's more, you can catch any breeze coming off the water. You may be tempted to stay all day but, remember, you are not quite at the half-way point.

When you resume your walk, the trail takes an undulating course along the west side of the lake and after about ten minutes, descends to a large rock where there is a sign saying, "Bear right." It's a bit misleading—we did just this and got lost! Rather than merely bearing right, you must make a very sharp right turn (a hair-pin bend) then make a very steep, rocky descent to a bridge that takes you over wet ground at the end of an inlet.

A steep path rises on the other side, passing through trees. Soon after water comes into view on your right, you descend to cross a beaver dam. The trail then veers right and ascends a rocky outcrop. You soon reach open country where once again, the rocky path follows the line of the lake northwards, passing scattered clumps of juniper and small stands of pine and staghorn sumac. All the while, there are wonderful views over the narrow northern arm of the lake.

About 40 minutes past the resting place, you reach North Slide Junction. Take the right fork. The path takes you toward the sound of water and, after a minute or two, brings you to a bridge that crosses a fast stream, tumbling over rocks on its way to Slide Lake. A steep ascent takes you to a rocky outcrop and brings you out facing the most northerly stretch of Slide Lake. The trail heads north once again but, after a few minutes, starts to descend and to wind around the head of the lake.

As soon as you have made the turn to the south, the trail once more begins an upward slope, but this time through tall trees. You are now at the start of a journey along the narrow piece of land that separates Slide and Buck Lakes. After just a few minutes, you emerge from the trees to a fine outlook over Buck Lake.

The trail passes along the edge of a very dramatic rock face, then it continues south over sharply rising and falling terrain, before making a very steep descent. It then turns right, toward Slide Lake. (At this point you are crossing the short portage between the two lakes.) The trail veers south once more and, after about five minutes, you again hear the sound of water. Soon you reach the pretty stream that tumbles down the short, rocky stretch of ground between Slide and Buck Lakes. The trail crosses the cascade via a rustic bridge, and brings you down to the edge of Buck Lake. This is the spot where a log slide used to carry logs on their journey from Big Clear and Labelle Lakes into Buck Lake and onward to the mills on Mississauga Creek.

After crossing the stream, the trail continues south and, for the next 500 metres, leads you along the top of a narrow ridge that separates the two lakes. Gradually, the strip of land becomes wider, the terrain flatter. The path broadens as it begins to pass through very tall and mature trees. About an hour after North Slide Junction, you reach the trails leading left to the Buck Lake campsite. If the campsite is vacant, this is the perfect place for a final breather.

Back on the trail, you soon pass into more open countryside and, after ten minutes or so, you see water ahead on your right. You are approaching Ken Kellar's Pond, a very large beaver pond that has been in existence since the 1950s. There is a small precipitous section to negotiate as you pass round the edge, then you cross open meadow again to reach the sign at South Slide Junction.

The trek back to your car will take just under an hour, but you know the way now, so the return will probably seem shorter than the outward journey. In any event, your tiredness will be held at bay by the glow of satisfaction at having successfully completed a very challenging hike!

Gould Lake Conservation Area

Trail Information: Gould Lake Conservation Area has a 10-kilometre network of trails.

Rideau–Gould Lake Trails—13-kilometre linear trail, 5–6 hours, moderate to strenuous

Access: From Highway 401, exit north on to County Road 9 (exit #613). County Road 9 ends when it meets Rutledge Road. Turn left onto Rutledge Road and after about 2 kilometres, turn right, following Conservation Area signs, through Sydenham. Just north of Sydenham, look for Conservation Area signs on the left. Visitors must pay a fee.

Map: The *Rideau Trail Guidebook* contains an excellent map and descriptions of all the trails in Gould Lake Conservation Area.

Parking: The Gould Lake trail network can be accessed from the conservation area parking lot. See below for roadside parking to access the Rideau Trail.

Gould Lake Conservation Area, immediately to the south of Frontenac Provincial Park, is a wilderness area of rugged, rocky knolls and numerous intervening gullies. Swamps and beaver ponds are abundant in the low-lying areas. Its mature hardwoods —sugar maple, red oak, American beech and white birch—cast a deep, cool shade in spring and summer, and burst into a display of blazing colour in the fall. Here, you will find a network of diverse trails. Access to some easy trails, an excellent sandy beach and a grassy picnic area makes this an ideal spot for a family hike; however, there are also challenges for the more experienced hiker, particularly along the Rideau Trail, which passes through the area, following the eastern edge of Gould Lake.

A wonderfully scenic hike is one that starts near the north end of Gould Lake, where the Rideau Trail meets Bedford Road. It takes you south along the east shoreline to the picnic area at the end of the lake; then, following the conservation area trails, it hugs the west shoreline for 2.5 kilometres, before heading back toward

Rideau Valley

13

Bedford Road. The distance is about 13 kilometres. However, since the trail emerges onto Bedford Road about 3.5 kilometres south of the starting point, the hike is easier if you can use two cars and avoid a long walk along the road at the end.

Rideau–Gould Lake Trails

There are three points of access to the Gould Lake Side Trails from the stretch of Bedford Road north of Sydenham and just south of its intersection with the Salmon Lake Road entrance to Frontenac Provincial Park. They are not easy to find (a small sign and a blue triangle on a tree on the west side of the road is the only identification) so you have to keep a sharp lookout. If you are travelling south, you'll find East Trail 2.9 kilometres south of the intersection of Bedford Road and Salmon Lake Road. Famous Trail is 600 metres south of East Trail, and Wagon Trail is 800 metres further south (between McKercher Lane and Schultz Lane). If you are travelling north, to locate Wagon Trail, start looking out for Shultz Lane as soon as you have passed signs to Little Long Lake Road. (You'll find Famous Trail 800 metres north and East Trail 600 metres beyond that.)

It is a great help on to have two cars on this hike. Leave one car on the shoulder of Bedford Road (there are convenient spots on the road shoulder between East Trail and Famous Trail) and drive north along County Road 19 to a point about 300 metres past the Big Salmon Lake Road intersection. You should be able to see the orange Rideau Trail markers on the left. There is a good place to park on the right, 200 metres or so further on.

A sign at the access point tells you that you are on the Rideau Trail, Map 3, section 11. The path follows a wide track southeast. After a couple of hundred metres, it veers to the left, travelling through hardwood bush. After about 15 minutes you'll notice that the ground is becoming rockier and the bush is thinning out, giving way to rock-hugging junipers. Five minutes later, water comes into view to your left, and you soon get a fine view down the lake, which is dotted with small islands. The tree cover is a characteristic mixture of deciduous and conifer. In the fall, the view from here is a patchwork of blazing reds, vibrant yellows and dark-green, almost black.

When the trail reaches the lake, it swings right, over some logs, and starts to ascend to follow the shoreline from a somewhat

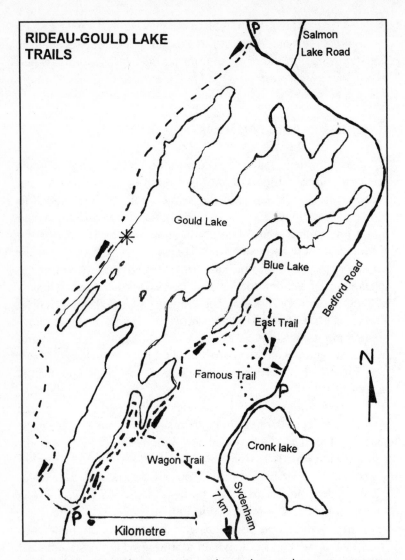

Salmon
Lake Road

Gould Lake

Blue Lake

Bedford Road

East Trail

Famous Trail

N

P

Cronk lake

Wagon Trail

7 km

Sydenham

Kilometre

elevated position. The terrain is rocky and rugged as you pass over lichen-covered boulders. But there is plenty of vegetation in the soil pockets between the rocks—in late summer and fall you'll find quite a show of golden rod and aster.

As the trail continues to climb, the views over the lake get better all the time. After reaching a grassy knoll, the path starts a fairly sharp descent to lake level, where it skirts a tiny inlet. Logs have been laid to take you over a wet section here.

Follow the trail's undulating course along the shoreline, and after walking for a little over an hour, you'll find yourself almost level with a small group of islands. You then pass through a Rideau

Rideau Valley

Trail primitive campsite and, about ten minutes later, just after you have skirted a pond, you pass a couple of mica pits (the second is almost a cave). Some of the granite rocks hereabouts have a distinctive pink colour; all in all, this is a lovely portion of trail. Silver birch and large pine form a graceful backdrop, luxuriant ferns proliferate between the jumbled rocks, and water lilies blanket the shallow waters on the right side of the trail. The path can be quite wet here; at one point you have to navigate your way around a stream and a breached beaver dam.

After leaving the wet area, the trail rises to pass along the top of a rocky ridge. Here, the path is marked by cairns rather than markers, but it is not hard to follow. To the left you look out over a very long, narrow inlet to a slim spit of land jutting into the lake.

A little further on, the trail climbs quite steeply through a rocky gully, alongside a stream. After crossing the stream, the path veers left, ascending to a high, rocky plateau, where there are excellent views over the tops of the trees. However, as you approach the south end of the lake, you begin to look down onto wetland and what's more, you realize it has to be crossed! Start preparing for a challenge!

The trail makes a quick descent down the side of a gully to a very large, very wet area. On your way down, be sure to pick up a stout stick, if don't already have one. Conveniently placed, downed trees afford the best way of making your way across the swamp, but you'll need a stick for balance.

Beyond the swamp, the trail crosses a second gully (this one is not too wet) and, a little further on, a boardwalk takes you over wetland in a third gully. After another ten minutes, you reach Hill Junction, in just a couple more minutes you'll catch a glimpse of the lake ahead. The Marion Webb Boardwalk takes you over a marsh, then, after five minutes, the trail (which by now is a wide, flat path) passes the pit of an old mica mine. A hundred metres more and you are at the beach, having covered about 9 kilometres of intermittently strenuous hiking.

However, you have now reached the perfect place for a lunch stop—picnic tables, a splendid view north over the lake and, in case you need to cool off, a fine, sandy swimming area.

The Tom Dixon Trail is named in memory of a student who drowned in 1971 while helping to build a trail. It begins at the barn and, according to the Rideau Trail Guide, it "ascends a steep slope and descends back to just above lake level." When I did this walk, my group missed the start of the trail. From the rear of the barn, we took a road from the end of the parking area heading west through tall, mature hardwoods. When it failed to ascend, as promised, we nevertheless continued (it takes a gently undulating course through delightful woods) and after about 15 minutes we veered left along an unmarked path that emerged, after a further ten minutes, at the lake edge and joined the Tom Dixon Trail. Obviously, this is a slightly unorthodox but easy way to access the Tom Dixon Trail.

From here, the trail pursues its undulating course northwards, following the shoreline along a spit of land that forms the south side of a narrow channel separating the main body of Gould Lake from a large bay. Just before it reaches the end of the spit, the trail makes a very sharp turn to head back south, along the east side of the spit. After crossing a bridge over a creek, you arrive at a major intersection of trails—Porky Junction (it takes 50 minutes to an hour from the barn to reach this point). Don't get confused here. The Tom Dixon Trail turns to head north. (The trail heading east is the Wagon Trail, a 1.3-kilometre trail that can be used as a shortcut to Desert Lake Road, if you've had enough.)

After hugging the bayou-like shoreline for a 100 metres or so, the path starts to climb. It takes you to the top of a cliff, where you can look down on the lake through the trees. Then there is a very steep descent. Shortly after you reach the bottom, there is another intersection. Keep right. After 200 metres, the Tom Dixon Trail ends at an intersection called Mica Junction. Here, you veer right on the East Trail, which takes you 100 metres through a dense hemlock grove to Famous Junction. From here, either Famous Trail or East Trail will take you back to Desert Lake Road and your car.

Foley Mountain Conservation Area

Trail Information: Foley Mountain Conservation Area has a 14-kilometre network of trails.

Rideau–Foley Mountain Trails—6-kilometre loop, 2 hours, easy to moderate

Access: From Westport, drive 0.4 kilometres north on County Road 10. Turn east into Foley Mountain Conservation Area. Visitors must pay a fee.

Map: A map showing the trails is available at the registration point.

Parking: Near the entrance to the conservation area.

A geological fault runs along the north shore of the Upper Rideau Lake, separating the Precambrian rocks of the Frontenac Axis from younger, Paleozoic rocks on the south shore of the lake. Foley Mountain Conservation Area occupies a stunning position, overlooking Upper Rideau Lake, right on the top of the 65-metre escarpment that marks the fault. Within its 325 hectares of forest, ponds and fields, you'll find a variety of walks and some breathtaking views. The area is covered by a number of trails. Blue-blazed Conservation Area trails explore both the escarpment and the flatter ground away from the edge. The most rugged hiking is along the Rideau Trail, which passes through the area, and the most satisfying hikes are those that combine sections of the Rideau with some of the Conservation Area trails. Foley Mountain Conservation Area is an ideal place for the neophyte to get a brief experience of hiking on the Canadian Shield.

Settlement of the area that became Westport started early in the nineteenth century. It had a sawmill by 1817 and gradually grew to become a focal point of commerce along the Rideau waterway system. In its heyday, it had a couple of feed mills, a tannery, a foundry, a woollen mill and five blacksmiths. The Brockville, Westport and Sault Ste. Marie Railway ended here when the money to build it ran out. (The railway station still stands, on Highway 42.) Today, its scenic location and its historic sites and buildings attract thousands of tourists.

Rideau Valley

Westport, or Morison's Mills, at West end of Upper Rideau Lake.

Westport in 1934, one of a series of 114 watercolours by
Thomas Burrows, Assistant Overseer of Works for the Rideau Canal.
Source: Archives of Ontario, C1-0-0-0-28

You'll appreciate just why it's so popular when you get to Spy Rock, a lookout point a few metres west of the car park at the top of Foley Mountain. On your right, the escarpment makes a wide sweep around the north shore of Westport Sand Lake, while directly below is the Upper Rideau Lake and the village, aptly named in reference to its position at the lake's western end.

On a fine day, you look down on an idyllic scene. Tucked into a triangle of flat land between the waters of Rideau Lake, Westport Pond and Westport Sand Lake, Westport's houses, some limestone, some white-washed, are scattered in picturesque disarray among groves of tall deciduous trees. Only church spires and a water tower rise above the level of the treetops. A little further off, on the more amenable soils, farmhouses and barns dot a gently rolling landscape of fields and meadows, and, beyond that, ridge upon ridge of trees stretch out to the horizon.

Rideau–Foley Mountain Trails

When you leave Spy Rock, follow the blue markers of Scenic Ridge Trail east, along the line of the escarpment. After about 400 metres on the winding, rocky path, you come to an opening in the trees on the right with a great view over Upper Rideau Lake and the countryside to the east. Continue along the blue-marked trail, over pink humpbacked rocks, and when you reach a sign to the parking area, keep right, along a path that heads toward the lake, descending slightly. After five minutes you come to a sign pointing down the hill to the Rockslide Lookout. A very steep, short trail leads to a vantage point above a section of jumbled rock and scree. If you are tempted to explore, be warned that the return journey is quite a scramble that can be difficult in wet weather.

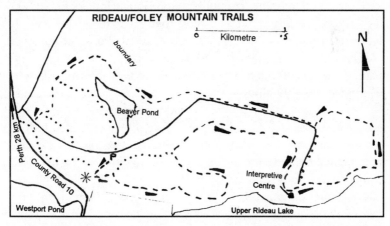

Continuing on the blue trail, you pass another lookout after a couple of minutes. Then the path curves to the left, starts to ascend and, after about ten minutes, brings you to another parking area sign. Keep right and, in a couple of minutes, when you come to an intersection, turn right to follow the orange triangles of the Rideau Trail. Almost immediately, you will find a rather old and decrepit boardwalk designed to take you across a swampy area. (In places it has sunk, so the crossing can be a bit dicey.)

Next you come to a tricky section where there seems to be a plethora of markers. When you see blue and orange markers on the same tree, stop and look carefully for the next plain orange marker, more or less ahead. Don't make the mistake of following orange markers with a yellow tip—they are heading the wrong way! If you are heading east through hardwood forest, following plain orange markers, you are on the correct trail. After about

500 metres, you reach an intersection. Take the right fork—a blue-blazed trail that descends quite steeply through trees for 500 metres to bring you to the Interpretive Centre. A short trail leads east from here to the beach. By now you have covered about three kilometres, so if it is a hot day, picnic tables and a sandy swimming area make this is the perfect spot for a lunch break.

From the beach, you have a choice of routes to start the homeward trek. You can either take the gravel road that climbs from the beach parking area, or, at the east end of the beach, look for the yellow-tipped triangles of the Rideau Trail, which makes a slightly more strenuous ascent of the escarpment. The trails meet at the top and, from this point, you head west on a gravel road, the Gough Trail. If you are ready for home, keep on the Gough Trail for about 1 kilometre to reach the parking lot.

If you're up for more, continue on the Gough Trail for about 600 metres until, on your right, you see a road marked "private" which leads to to the park supervisor's house. Just beyond, at an open area, you'll see blue markers leading into the bush on the right. The path takes you through a grassy meadow and into trees before veering to the right along a fence line.

The trail continues to make a wide curve round to the west, taking you past an enormous, very old maple and, a little further on, an equally ancient white pine. The trail passes through a young pine plantation and soon meets a trail coming in from the left. This is the Beaver Pond Trail. If you follow it southeast it will take you past a beaver pond and back to the Gough Trail. Alternatively, you can carry on across a small bridge, following the numbered signs of the Beaver Pond Trail to a tree marked with the number 10. Again you have a choice. You can bear left and follow the Beaver Pond Trail south, first over rocky ground, then alongside a beaver meadow. It joins the Gough Trail after about 400 metres. If you keep right, you'll get to the Gough Trail after about 100 metres. Either way, you'll be back at the car park in less than ten minutes.

Murphys Point Provincial Park

Trail Information: Murphys Point Provincial Park has a 15-kilometre network of trails.

Murphys Point Loop—7-kilometre loop, 2–3 hours, easy to moderate

Access: From Perth, drive south on County Road 1 for about 8 kilometres. Turn right onto Elm Grove Road (County Road 21). After about 11 kilometres, you will see the entrance to Murphys Point Provincial Park on the left. Park users must pay a fee.

Map: A Hiking Trail Guide is available from the park office.

Parking: At the boat launch parking area

Murphys Point Provincial Park juts out into the waters of Big Rideau Lake. Its position, on the Rideau Canal between Rideau Ferry and Narrows Lock 18 kilometres south of the town of Perth, puts it at the heart of a very popular tourist area. Sandy beaches, superb boating and fishing facilities, and two large campgrounds complete with washrooms, showers and laundry facilities make this an ideal park for families. During the summer season, there are many special programs: evening presentations by guest speakers and the park's naturalists, a special series of activities for children and many guided hikes along the park's hiking trails.

Gregariousness, however, is not mandatory. If you prefer to be away from the crowds you can canoe or hike into one of several small campsites at the water's edge. You won't be in the wilderness, but you'll be pretty much on your own. The same is true of the park trails; with a wee bit of planning, you can get away from people to explore in solitude.

Don't be fooled by the park's size. Yes, it is small compared with Frontenac, but you will nonetheless find an amazingly rich and varied mixture of sights, sounds and experiences. If your time is limited, you can do no better than to let Murphys Point give you an unforgettable introduction, not only to the natural beauty of this corner of the Canadian Shield but also to the lives of the people who had the temerity to settle here.

Rideau Valley

Here, as in the other parks along the Rideau Trail, geology has helped to create a wonderfully diverse landscape. Along the shoreline, windswept rocky promontories open onto panoramic views over wide expanses of water. As in typical northern forests, spruce, balsam and fir exist side by side with mixed forest of maple, beech, white ash and oak. Wetlands offer sanctuary to many species of birds, and, around the old homesteads, there are long-abandoned fields, now being reclaimed by sumac, prickly ash and hawthorn.

The park's hiking trails are equally diverse. Two of the easiest and most popular ones explore Ontario's past. The McParlan Trail winds along the forested shoreline of Hogg Bay to the mouth of Black Creek and the ruins of the Burgess sawmill, built in 1810. Nearby is McParlan House, a restored log home, one of the earliest log buildings in the area. (It predates the founding of the town of Perth by four years.)

Try not to miss the hike to the Silver Queen Mine. Along the road, about 3 kilometres southwest of the park entrance, an easy trail leads from the Lally Homestead to the Silver Queen Mine. Between 1903 and 1920, mica, apatite and feldspar were extracted from this mine, which is a typical example of the many small-scale mining operations that took place on the southern Canadian Shield. Along the route, interpretive plaques describe the mining process and the mine's history; however, if you can, try to visit this site in the summer and take the guided tour. (I'm not usually one for guided tours, but this one I heartily recommend.) This is the only mine in this area that has been preserved and opened to the public, and the tour that takes you 25 metres below the surface to the main mine shaft and on to the restored bunkhouse is fascinating.

My favourite hike is one that winds around Murphys Point, the peninsula that juts into Big Rideau Lake. It is neither rugged nor particularly strenuous, but it's wonderfully varied and it takes you to some marvellous lookouts over the water.

Murphys Point Loop

Start from the parking area at the main boat launch. A hiking icon at the end of the parking lot marks the beginning of the Rocky Narrows Trail, heading northeast through trees. After about five minutes, the path, which is soft and leafy underfoot, passes through a couple of stands of hemlock—after rain they give off a wonderful, pungent perfume—before entering mature mixed forest. Now and

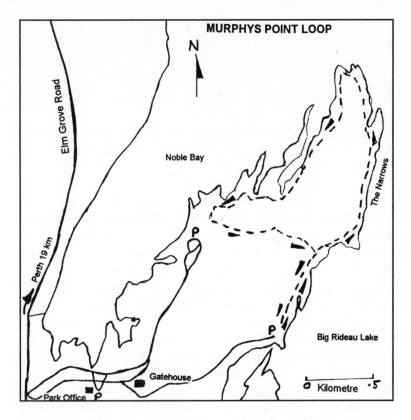

N

Elm Grove Road

Perth 19 km

Noble Bay

The Narrows

P

P

Big Rideau Lake

P

Gatehouse

Park Office P

0 Kilometre .5

again, you will glimpse water on your right. After a short 15 minutes, the trail brings you quite close to the water, to meet the Point Trail. Keep right, heading toward the water and, after a minute or so, you will reach a small sandy beach. It's a beautiful spot: a rocky promontory, a tiny offshore island just large to accommodate two cedars and a pine, and beyond, the open waters of Big Rideau Lake stretching out to the south. I was there on a very hot day in late July; admittedly it was midweek, but apart from one or two large boats, from where I stood there was no other sign of human presence.

At the beach, the trail veers sharp left (look for the icon) into tall woods and, after about ten minutes, approaches the water once again. The path continues north, never very far from the shore, through deciduous forest. You know you are approaching the end of the peninsula when you begin to glimpse water ahead, as well as on the right. The trail crosses a gully and meets the shore at a very sheltered spot where water lilies carpet the surface of the lake. In a minute or two, you reach Murphys Point—a pine-studded, grassy clearing, sloping toward the water. Off the point the water is

Rideau Valley

a bit reedy, so it's perhaps not great for swimming, but the point is a wonderful place for a picnic. The lake is narrower here, and you can see cottages on the opposite bank, but they are well back from the water so they are not intrusive. Boats dot the lake. However, as docking is not allowed along the peninsula shoreline, this vantage point is very quiet.

From Murphys Point, the trail travels south for about a kilometre, never far from the water, until it brings you to a high rocky outcrop overlooking a very dark and shady inlet. Here it meets the Sylvan Trail. Keep right and, after about five minutes, the trail will bring you into much taller, more mature hardwoods. On a hot day, the Sylvan Trail is especially delightful; the tall trees have an airy feel to them, luxuriant green ferns line the path and the high canopy casts shimmering patterns of light and shade. If you are there in spring or early summer, your progress is almost certain to be accompanied by a lively chorus of many songbirds, particularly the numerous warblers that make their home in the canopy.

The trail gradually swings south and then east, making a loop around the middle of the peninsula, and taking you past the day use area of the park and along the edge of Fallows Campground. Each time you come to an intersection, keep left.

But when you reach the sign to Rocky Narrows beach, keep right. After a few moments the trail divides again; the right fork takes you straight back to your starting point, the left goes down to the little beach. If it's a hot day, you might want to do as I did, and end it with a swim. More likely than not, you'll be alone; the water will be cool and clear, the sand firm, and it will take about three minutes to swim out to the island. There, you can stretch out on the rocks and take in the breathtaking panorama of the south arm of Big Rideau Lake. After three hours or so on the trail, it's the perfect way to conclude a delightful hike.

Other Rideau Valley Trails

Although some of the hikes in this region take you along short sections of the Rideau Trail, the descriptions here give just the merest hint of what the trail has to offer. Between Kingston and Ottawa, 387 kilometres of cleared, marked trail await the hiker. Where the trail traverses the Frontenac Axis of the Shield, there are some great opportunities for rugged hiking. Although there are few looped sections along the way, day hiking becomes feasible if you have two cars. To explore the trail satisfactorily, you must have a copy of the Rideau Trail Guidebook. For information on how to become a member of the Rideau Trail Association or to obtain a guidebook, call (613) 545-0823.

Situated west of Highway 38, north of Verona, **Depot Lakes Conservation Area** has 85 drive-in campsites, some canoe-in sites, and 9 kilometres of hiking trails. To get there from Highway 38, take Snider Road west for about 9 kilometres. For information call (613) 374-2940.

Highway 38 closely follows the route of the old Kingston and Pembroke Railway, one of the railway lines that opened up isolated areas that had thwarted the earlier road builders. Opened in 1884, to transport lumber and iron from isolated camps and mines, it also carried passengers and supplies between Kingston and Renfrew. As its name suggests, it was supposed to run as far as Pembroke, but it never made it past Renfrew. When the supplies of lumber and iron ran out, the railway continued to bring vacationers to small resorts such as Sharbot Lake and Calabogie. Its passengers found the twisting, undulating route so slow that the railway was nicknamed the "Kick and Push." In any event, it staggered on until 1959. The rail tracks were removed in 1966 and, in 1972, the Mississippi Valley Conservation Area opened 40 kilometres of railbed, (the K & P Trail) between Snow Road Station and Barryvale, as a recreational trail for hikers, mountain bikers and motorized vehicles.

I'm usually not much taken with multi-use trails, but this one does pass through some exceptionally fine country. In *Hiking Ontario's Heartland*, Shirley Teasdale particularly recommends the 14-kilometre stretch between Lavant Station and Flower Station, while Ron Brown, in *Ghost Railways of Ontario*, regards the section between Flower Station and Barryvale as the most scenic. Whichever bit you choose, you'll go by marshes and tiny lakes, and pass through the silent remains of the once-bustling towns and

Rideau Valley

147

villages that lined the route of the K&P. To try it, take Highway 511 north from Lanark. Turn west onto County Road 16, and follow it to Lavant Station. The trail is marked by a large Conservation Area sign.

Frontenac Park, (613) 376-3489, has wonderful wilderness campsites for those who like to canoe or hike in to their destination. Drive-in campsites are available at Depot Lakes Conservation Area, off Highway 38 (see above), also at Murphys Point Provincial Park, (613) 267-5060, and along Highway 7 at Silver Lake Provincial Park, (613) 268-2000, and Sharbot Lake Provincial Park, (613) 335-2814. See page 149 for more useful contact numbers.

As I like to combine my hikes with very good food and a great deal of comfort, I am always on the lookout for exceptional places to stay. I have found the perfect place near Frontenac Park; so perfect, in fact, that I'm almost reluctant to share my secret. But here it is.

Drive north from the park on Bedford Road. When the main road swings left toward Verona, keep heading north on Bedford Road. After about 9 kilometres, on your right, you pass a side road. One kilometre beyond this junction, you'll see Deerwood Farm on your left. It's unique. Two century-old log cabins have been creatively combined to form a long, low farmhouse, set in rolling field and forest. There are four bedrooms and two bathrooms for guests, and a guest sitting-room. Sandie and Don Ash, the owners, and their black lab, Macallan, will give you the warmest of welcomes. The breakfasts are great—enough to keep you going all day—but Sandie's dinners are something to rave about. After a hard day's hiking, Deerwood farm is a dream come true. For more information call (613) 273-4412.

Information Sources

Provincial Parks

www.Ontarioparks.com
Camping Reservations
for Provincial Parks
1-888-ONT-PARK

Algonquin Provincial Park
(705) 633-5572

Awenda Provincial Park
(705) 549-2231

Arrowhead Provincial Park
(705) 789-5105

Bon Echo Provincial Park
(613) 336-2228

Frontenac Provincial Park
(613) 376-3489

Killbear Provincial Park
(705) 342-5492

Murphys Point Provincial Park
(613) 267-5060

Petroglyphs Provincial Park
(705) 877-2552

Silent Lake Provincial Park
(613) 339-2807

The Massasauga
Provincial Park
(705) 378-2401

Other Parks and Recreation Areas

Foley Mountain
Conservation Area
(613) 692-3571

Leslie M. Frost Natural
Resources Centre
(705) 766-2451

Georgian Bay Islands
National Park
(705) 756-2415
www.parkscanada.pch.gc.ca
Camping Reservations
(705) 756-5909

Gould Lake Conservation Area
(613) 546-9965

Tourism and Accommodation

Bancroft & District
Chamber of Commerce
(613) 332-1513

Bracebridge Chamber
of Commerce
(705) 645-5231

Bracebridge Visitor
Information Centre
(705) 645-8121

Gravenhurst Chamber
of Commerce
(705) 687-4432

Haliburton Highlands
Chamber of Commerce
1-800-461-7677
www.Haliburtonhighlands.com

Huntsville & Lake of Bays
Chamber of Commerce
(705) 789-4771

Land O'Lakes Tourist
Association
(613) 336-8818
www.lol.on.ca

Muskoka Tourism
1-800-267-9700
www.traveltomuskoka.com

Parry Sound Chamber
of Commerce
(705) 746-4213
1-800-461-4261

Parry Sound Area Tourism
(705) 746-4455

Penetang–Tiny Chamber
of Commerce
(705) 549-2232
1-800-263-7745

Westport & Rideau Lakes
Chamber of Commerce
(613) 272-2929
www.westportrideaulakes.on.ca

Bed & Breakfast Associations

Lanark County Bed &
Breakfast Association
(613) 256-3692

Leeds & Grenville Bed &
Breakfast Accommodation
(613) 273-7848

Muskoka Bed & Breakfast
www.BBmuskoka.com

Cottage Rental

Cottages Unlimited Realty
(613) 284-0400
www.cottagesunlimited.com

Vacationtime Realty
(705) 687-0066
www.vacationtimerealty.com

Resorts

Resorts Ontario
1-800-363-7227
www.resorts-ontario.com

Information Sources

Bibliography

Barber, Christian, and Fuchs, Terry. *Their Enduring Spirit: The History of Frontenac Provincial Park 1783–1990.* Kingston, Ontario: Quarry Press, 1997.

Brown, Ron. *Ghost Towns of Ontario.* Toronto: Polar Bear Press, 1997.

———. *Ghost Railways of Ontario.* Toronto: Polar Bear Press, 1998.

Callan, Kevin. *Cottage Country Canoe Routes.* Erin, Ontario: Boston Mills Press, 1993.

Carpenter, Donna Gibbs. *Daytripper 3—50 Trips In and Around Eastern Ontario.* Erin, Ontario: Boston Mills Press, 1994.

———. *Daytripper 4—50 Trips In Ontario Cottage Country.* Erin, Ontario: Boston Mills Press, 1996.

Chambers, Brenda, et al. *Forest Plants of Central Ontario.* Edmonton, Alberta: Lone Pine Publishing, 1996.

Chapman, L.T., and Putnam D.F. *The Physiography of Southern Ontario.* Ministry of Natural Resources, 1984.

Fitsell, Bill and Dawber, Michael. *Fitsell's Guide to the Old Ontario Strand.* Kingston, Ontario: Quarry Press, 1994.

Killan, Gerald. *Protected Places: A History of Ontario's Provincial Park System.* Toronto: Dundurn Press Ltd. in association with the Ministry of Natural Resources, 1993.

Long, Gary. *This River The Muskoka.* Erin, Ontario: Boston Mills Press, 1989.

Macfie, John. *Parry Sound: Logging Days.* Erin, Ontario: Boston Mills Press, 1992.

MacKay, Niall. *Over the Hills to Georgian Bay.* Erin, Ontario: Boston Mills Press, 1998.

Ministry of Northern Development and Mines. *ROCK ONtario.* Ontario: 1994

Murray, Florence B., ed. *Muskoka and Haliburton, 1615–1875: a Collection of Documents.* Toronto: University of Toronto Press, 1963.

Niering, William A. and Olmstead, Nancy C. *The Audubon Society Field Guide to North American Wildflowers.* New York: Alfred A. Knopf Inc., 1979.

Perkins, Mary Ellen, comp. *A Guide to Provincial Plaques in Ontario.* Toronto: Natural Heritage/Natural History Inc., Ministry of Culture and Communications, 1989

Rideau Trail Association. *The Rideau Trail Guidebook,* 4th Edition. 1995

Roberts, David C. *A Field Guide to Geology: Eastern North America.* New York: Houghton Mifflin Company, 1996.

Runtz, Michael. *The Explorer's Guide to Algonquin Park.* Erin, Ontario: Boston Mills Press, reprint 2000.

Teasdale, Shirley. *Hiking Ontario's Heartland.* Vancouver: Whitecap, 1993.

Tozer, Ron, and Strickland, Dan. *A Pictorial History of Algonquin Park.* Whitney, Ontario: The Friends of Algonquin Park and the Ministry of Natural Resources, 1991.

Wake, Winifred (Cairns), ed. *A Nature Guide to Ontario.* Toronto: University of Toronto Press, 1997.

Bibliography

Index of Place Names

Index of Place Nmaes

Hiking Notes